D1468676

Single No More

How and Where to Meet Your Perfect Mate

ELLEN KREIDMAN, PH.D.

RENAISSANCE BOOKS

Los Angeles

Library of Congress Cataloging-in-Publication Data

Kreidman, Ellen.
   Single no more / Ellen Kreidman.
        p.   cm.
   ISBN 1-58063-078-2 (alk. paper)
   1. Mate selection. 2. Dating (Social customs). 3. Man-woman relationships.
   4. Single people—Psychology. I. Title.
   HQ801.K724   1999
   646.7'7—dc21   99-19598
                                                                                  CIP

10 9 8 7 6 5 4 3 2 1

Design by Lisa-Theresa Lenthall
Typesetting by Jesus Arellano

Distributed by St. Martin's Press
Manufactured in the United States of America
First Edition

JUN   1999

This book is dedicated to my husband, Steve, who has given me the greatest gift of all: the opportunity to love and be loved with total and complete devotion. I am the luckiest woman alive to have the honor of being your wife. You are my inspiration, my rock, my perfect mate. You are my world. Thank you for a lifetime of happiness.

Contents

I am forever grateful to the following people in my life:

My parents, who provided me with an environment where I could reach, stretch, and grow.

Martha Wolf, a mother every daughter dreams of having. Her good nature, compassion, and optimism have touched my life in many ways.

My children, Tara, Tiffany, and Jason, who have given me so much happiness and so many reasons to be proud. Not a day goes by that I don't feel blessed and privileged to be their mother.

My brother Harvey and sister-in-law Susan, who have given me their love and support and have made me a proud aunt to their beautiful children, Matthew and Allison.

My sister-in-law Barbara, who is kind, understanding, and a great supporter of my work.

Frankie Wright, whose friendship, encouragement, and support not only enriches my life, but the lives of everyone she comes in contact with.

Bill Hartley, still "the Chairman of the Universe," whose brilliant and intuitive mind as an editor helped sharpen and enhance my manuscript. As my publisher, his wisdom, experience, guidance, and patience are a constant source of inspiration. Most important, on a personal level he is a kind and compassionate man, who has touched my life deeply.

Kathy Dawson, "the First Lady of Motivation," who has helped thousands of couples find greater happiness and put more romance into their lives. Her endless hours of dedication, energy, and creative talents are always a labor of love. The stories she contributed gave life to my concepts, thoughts, and ideas.

Sandra Caton, whose remarkable insights and outstanding literary talents added focus and clarity to my manuscript.

Michael Dougherty, Director of Marketing and Sales for Renaissance Books, whose constant optimism, never-ending encouragement, and pure professionalism turns possibilities into probabilities. He is truly a class act when it comes to promoting and marketing my work.

Kathryn Mills, my publicist, whose enthusiasm is contagious. Her dedication and ability to give of herself both personally and professionally go far beyond any job description. When it comes to handling an author's busy schedule, she does it with style and grace.

The thousands of men and women who have opened their hearts and shared their experiences with me. Without them this book could not have been written.

And most of all to God, for my continued good health and the opportunity to "be of most benefit."

TAKE CONTROL OF YOUR LOVE LIFE

Congratulations! By purchasing this book, you have shown you're ready to find the love of your life. Whether you are newly single or have been searching for a mate for a long time, this book will show how and where to meet your perfect partner.

I believe the most important reason for living is to love someone with all your heart and to have that person love you back. *Single No More* is my gift to all of you who truly want to be able to give and receive love in a warm, supportive, and healthy relationship. Everyone deserves to experience that!

With this book, you'll have complete control over your love life. Instead of sitting around waiting for that special someone to fall out of the sky and into your lap, you'll know just how to find the perfect match for you.

If you needed a job, you wouldn't wait for opportunity to come knocking at your door. Successful people don't rely on luck to get a job, they take action. They use all the job-hunting techniques. They update their résumé, check out the "Want Ads," surf the Internet, network with associates and friends, and contact employment agencies. Everyone I know who has a successful career is action-oriented. They didn't wait around for the perfect job to magically appear. They worked for it.

Finding a mate isn't any different. Why should finding someone to share your life with be easier than finding a job? Shouldn't you be willing to devote more effort, energy, and commitment to finding a life partner than finding a job? After all, marriage is meant to last "as long as you both shall live." I don't know anyone who makes that kind of commitment when taking a job.

Most of us learned job-hunting skills in school, but there were no courses on finding the perfect mate or determining what type of person would be right for you.

A few generations ago, most women were satisfied with a man who could support them, and most men were happy with a woman who could cook and clean house. It's wonderful that today men and women expect more from their mates. But it means that finding a mate is more difficult. You have to actively search for the right person rather than settling for the first eligible person who comes along. The problem is, nobody taught us how.

DO THE WORK
AND REAP THE REWARDS

That's why I've written this book. In my long career as a relationship counselor, teacher, writer, and lecturer, I've been responsible for thousands of matches made in heaven. So many in fact, people refer to me as "The Fairy Godmother of Relationships." For over eighteen years, I've shown men and women how easy it is to meet the partner of their dreams. Along the way, I've collected love stories by the hundreds—true stories told to me by people who used my principles to change their lives. They were men and women of all ages, from every imaginable occupation, and background. What they had in common was their desire to love and be loved in a life-long relationship with a perfect mate. Although their names have been changed to protect their privacy, their personal stories, which I will share in the following pages, are all true. I hope these stories will motivate you to take the necessary steps to get the love you want and deserve.

By reading this book and taking the actions I describe, you will acquire the skills you need to find and attract the perfect mate. My part is the easy part—telling you exactly what to do to make that happen. Your part is the fun part—carrying out the instructions and reaping the rewards. As you read each chapter and complete the assignments, you will become more confident, secure, and happy, you will learn specific ways to find potential partners, and you will have more dates and choices than you ever dreamed possible.

Make no mistake—getting the relationship you want takes work. Before you even begin to look for your perfect partner you have to take a long, hard look at yourself. You will need a notebook or journal in which to answer the questions and complete the exercises assigned, and you will need to devote time to self-examination and self-improvement, as well as to the actual search for your perfect mate.

As you read this book:

- *Be open-minded*
  Some of the ideas in this book may be new to you. Consider the possibility of applying them to your own life.

- *Be willing to try*
  Let your new knowledge lead to action. Decide you will try new behaviors even though they may feel uncomfortable.

- *Be patient*
  Don't worry if you are unable or unwilling to apply the principles immediately. You may have to cover all the material before you are ready to begin making changes.

- *Be honest with yourself*
  If you find you've been making mistakes, admit them and be willing to change.

- *Share your search with a friend*
  Unlike job-hunting, where the first rule is to never take a friend along on an interview, reading this book and doing the exercises with a friend can make the process even more exciting. Having a friend involved can keep you on track, provide important feedback, and bolster your courage when you hit a stumbling block.

- *Have fun*
  With the right attitude, meeting new people, getting out of your rut, and trying new things can be fun. Give yourself permission to do the things you enjoy most as you search for your perfect partner.

LIFE IS SHORT

If you are currently in a relationship that is going nowhere, or you are with someone who is unwilling to make a commitment, please pay attention! Life is too short to be with someone who doesn't love you enough to stand at the altar and vow to stay with you for "as long as you both shall live." You don't have to settle for crumbs when you can have a feast. You don't have to settle for weeds when you can have a garden. Give up the waiting game and take action now to create the relationship of your dreams with the perfect partner for you. Join me on a journey that will help you learn from your past relationships, take pride in who you are right now, and make wiser choices in the future.

CHAPTER 1

You Deserve to Be Loved

BE PROUD OF WHO YOU ARE

In a world of change-your-life seminars, self-help books and tapes, and motivational gurus, where people are always "working on themselves," here's a bold, new, idea—be yourself. The best way to meet your perfect mate is to be who you really are, not who you think someone wants you to be. No matter what type of personality you have, it's yours, so be proud of it. Only by being yourself will you find someone who appreciates who you are. You don't have to change your personality. Being in a relationship where you have to pretend to be someone you're not is exhausting. You are a uniquely wonderful human being who deserves to be loved just as you are!

I can just hear you saying, "Wait a second. Isn't Ellen Kreidman a self-help speaker herself? Isn't she famous for her infomercials about improving your relationships?"

The answer is yes. I am a relationships expert; I have books and tapes; and I give seminars about changes you can make to improve your love life. But there are changes, and then there are changes.

We all learn new things and make changes every day. No doubt, all of us feel we can improve some aspect of ourselves, and I have some specific things to say about self-improvement later in this chapter. But right now, I want to deal with trying to be what you are not, in order to make someone like you.

As you live your life and grow into what might be called your "selfhood," you will have become a particular individual. There are certain things that you believe in your heart to be right or true, and you have ways of viewing and doing things that are personal to you. Some of them are just habits, but some are the very things that make you who you are. Whether they stem from natural abilities or learned responses, they have become so much a part of you that they define your personality.

It's perfectly appropriate to make a conscious decision to be a better listener, eat a healthier diet, or take dance lessons, but those kinds of changes are quite different from pretending to be someone you aren't. To try to change your core beliefs, your sense of personal morality, or something as intrinsic as your sense of humor so someone else will like you, is plain wrong. And it won't work. It won't get you the kind of person you can share your life with.

For example, if you're the kind of person who's the life of the party and you meet someone who is uncomfortable with an outgoing person, it would be like shooting yourself in the foot to act quiet and shy in order to be liked. Hiding your true self is sure to backfire. Nobody can put on an act forever. Sooner or later, the real you will emerge, and when it does, the person you've been fooling will feel betrayed. You don't have to put on an act for anybody.

If you've ever seen me on television or at one of my lectures, you know that I am a very outgoing, verbal person. I have always loved talking to people. When I was in elementary school, my teacher called me "motor mouth."

When my husband met me, he knew within minutes that I was very talkative. He soon learned I could talk to anyone, anywhere, anytime. I talked to people in movie lines, at the grocery store, waiting for a bus or train, anywhere at all, without the slightest provocation. My husband wasn't troubled by how friendly and outgoing I was. On the contrary, he told me it was refreshing to see someone so at ease around people. He said I seemed to really care about people, and that pleased him as well.

My husband was quite the opposite. He was not much of a talker and was shy and somewhat uncomfortable around people he didn't know. However, he was a great listener and very easygoing. He didn't get upset easily. I loved being with someone so patient, relaxed, and low-key. We were both being ourselves and were drawn to each other because we were comfortable with who we were. If we had tried to hide our true personalities in order to be more like each other, our relationship would never have gotten off the ground. Our personalities fit hand in glove, but if we hadn't been who we truly were, we would never have known that.

I believe the old saying, "Every pot has a cover." There is a perfect match for everyone, no matter what their personality.

For example, perhaps you see yourself as too emotional and believe you would be more lovable if you remained calm, cool and collected under all circumstances. Stop wishing you were different and understand you don't have to change a thing. You're perfect just the way you are. I assure you that eventually you will meet someone who loves the fact you live life in a passionate way and are deeply concerned about everyone.

If you tend to be a bit of a show-off, don't worry. Just relax and be your wonderful, entertaining self. Your perfect mate will love that you draw attention wherever you go and are the life of the party.

If you are quiet and introverted, don't feel you need to take a course in public speaking. Your perfect mate will love your calming and relaxing presence.

Be assured that when you meet the right person, you will feel comfortable and safe sharing your ideas and opinions, your likes and dislikes, your hopes and dreams, and your fears and disappointments. Sharing who you are and revealing yourself openly will make you feel special, loved, and accepted.

YOU ARE SPECIAL

No matter where you grew up or what social or economic background you come from, you are the sum of your own personal history. No one in the world has had the same experiences. Your background and life story make you a unique and valuable human being. To pretend you're anything else is to deny your own uniqueness.

Warren grew up on the farm in a loving, close-knit family. There was always food on the table and a roof overhead, but toys and new clothes were hard to come by. As a child, Warren wore hand-me-down clothes and was lucky if he had even one toy under the Christmas tree. As an adult, Warren craved financial success. He worked as a construction worker, but never felt he measured up to those who owned more than he did. He made a decent living but was unable to afford the cars and jewelry his higher-earning friends had.

When he met her, Warren wanted to impress Andrea. For their first date he borrowed his friend Sammy's new car and his friend Leon's leather jacket and Movado watch. It wasn't until their third date, when Warren couldn't borrow Sammy's car again, that he had to tell Andrea the truth. She felt so hurt and deceived she didn't want to see him again. She told Warren she wasn't upset because he didn't have a lot of money. What hurt was that he pretended to be something he wasn't.

Just because Warren didn't make as much money as his friends didn't mean he was less of a person. He was a hardworking man who grew up in a loving household. It was a mistake for him to think women would only be attracted to him if he were financially well off.

Josephine, who had been a waitress for over ten years, made a similar mistake. When she met Murray, she didn't want him to know she was a waitress, so she told him she worked for a restaurant chain. It wasn't exactly a lie, but it wasn't the truth either. Josephine hid the truth from Murray until one of his friends sat down at her table at the restaurant. Josephine had to wait on him, and when Murray learned Josephine was a waitress, he was very upset. When he confronted her, Murray told Josephine he felt hurt and angry at being deceived. He explained he liked her for who she was, not how she earned a living. Although it took several weeks, they were able to rebuild the trust in their relationship, and they've now been married for three years.

As Josephine learned, there is no reason to hide the truth. If what you do is more important to someone than who you are, why would you want that person's love?

BE TRUE TO YOURSELF

Being honest about who you are also means taking a stand when you feel strongly about something. Denying your feelings will only sabotage your efforts to meet your perfect mate.

Angela met Gregory at a friend's birthday party and was immediately attracted to him. She introduced herself and they began talking. After about half an hour, Gregory started telling ethnic jokes. With every joke he told, Gregory laughed harder. Angela knew her sense of humor was one of her strongest qualities, but she didn't find Gregory's jokes funny. She laughed politely at the first few jokes, then realized she couldn't pretend to be amused any longer. Even though she thought Gregory was attractive, she found his jokes offensive. Angela gently told Gregory she didn't find that kind of joke funny. They talked for a few more minutes, then she excused herself.

Angela knew herself well enough to know she wasn't comfortable around someone who made fun of another's ethnic background. She could have laughed along but stood by her principles and stayed true to herself.

If you really care about something, you don't need to pretend it's not important to you just because someone you met disagrees with you. Sooner or later, you'll find someone who feels the same way you do, or is at least open to learning more about your beliefs, ideas, values, or preferences.

For example, Ilene and Ralph met at a food booth at the county fair. Ilene was having trouble selecting something to eat that she considered healthy and commented on it to Ralph, who was standing in line next to her. Ralph laughed and said he was in heaven when he was in a setting like the fair, admitting that he was a fast-food junkie. Ilene was involved in an organic food co-op and tried very hard to eat healthy foods with no preservatives or pesticides. Ilene was very attracted to Ralph and knew if she expressed her feelings about organic food, she might make the situation uncomfortable, but she did it anyway. Ralph admitted he thought spending money on organic food was a waste but confessed he knew nothing about organic foods and probably wasn't a good judge. Ilene liked Raph's response and invited him to shop with her at the food co-op the following week. Ralph accepted and they had a wonderful afternoon.

Ilene had a split second to decide to be honest and tell Ralph how strongly she felt about eating organic foods. She stood up for what she believed and it led to a continuing relationship. If he had not been open to learning about organic food, their relationship might not have continued, but that would have been okay too, since they obviously wouldn't have been right for each other.

WHAT MATTERS TO YOU . . . MATTERS

If you take more than a few seconds to decide how to act when you're with someone, you're not being authentic. You know you're being yourself when you can spontaneously say whatever is in your heart or on your mind. Although you may risk losing that person's interest, if he or she is not comfortable with you, that person wouldn't be right for you anyway.

For example, Heather and her friends went to a party after work at a singles bar near the office. Heather ran into Todd, an attractive man she knew from her previous job. They were really enjoying their conversation about their jobs when Heather mentioned her volunteer work with an animal rescue organization, an activity that was really important to her. As she described the typical menagerie of animals she cared for as they recovered from various mishaps or waited for permanent homes, Todd quickly became disenchanted. He told Heather that animals weren't his thing, and politely excused himself. Even though she was surprised and disappointed, Heather was glad to have found out early that Todd wasn't interested in animals. She knew that if she and Todd had started dating, her houseful of dogs, cats, snakes, birds, turtles, and fish would eventually have become an issue in their relationship. She knew it would take being an avid animal lover for someone to become involved with her; and because she was being real, Heather discovered she and Todd were wrong for each other right away.

RESPECT YOURSELF

Here's another story about someone who learned that being yourself is best. Bob was in his early thirties and very self-conscious because he was rapidly losing his hair. He assumed no woman would be attracted to him without hair, so he wore a hat wherever he went. He met Sally at a friend's cookout and instantly fell in love. They sat in the shade and talked while they enjoyed hamburgers. Later in the afternoon, they joined a game of volleyball. It was a hot day and Bob's head was dripping, but there was no way he was going to take off his hat and let Sally see he was bald. On their second date Sally asked Bob why he never removed his hat. Bob responded that he was just a "hat kind of guy." After much coaxing, Bob finally took off his hat, certain their relationship was about to end. But Sally surprised him. When she saw his bald head, she exclaimed, "Oh, I love bald men! I think bald is so sexy!"

When you hide things about yourself, you're not only being dishonest, you're being disrespectful. I don't care if you're bald, heavier than you'd like to be, or have six toes! Respect yourself enough to reveal the real you. How else will your potential mate know you're perfect for him or her unless you are your authentic self and proud of who you are?

Neil was in his forties and never married. He loved children and wanted, more than anything, to find someone to spend the rest of his life with and raise a family. It wasn't important to him whether the children were his.

Mary was in her late thirties and was divorced with three children. She had been dating for two years but had yet to meet a man who wasn't put off by an instant family. She was beginning to think she should conceal that she had children when she met Neil at a mutual friend's retirement party. They talked for a couple of hours and really enjoyed themselves. When she mentioned her children, Neil surprised her with his enthusiasm. He told her his dream was to meet someone who loved children as much as he did. Mary showed Neil pictures of her children, and he asked if he could meet them someday. That someday was eight years ago, and now Neil has the family he dreamed of: Mary, her three children, and a child of their own.

THE TRUTH, THE WHOLE TRUTH, AND NOTHING BUT THE TRUTH

Remember, you have nothing to hide! No matter what it is, there's someone who will be attracted by the very thing you'd like to conceal. If you're pretending to be someone you're not, how will you ever know if the person you're attracted to cares about the true you or the person you're pretending to be?

Besides robbing yourself of the knowledge that you're liked for yourself, posing as something you're not requires all of your energy. You have to constantly monitor what you say to be sure you don't contradict something you said before. One lie leads to another, and before you know it, you're so tangled in a web of deceit you're not even sure who you are yourself. With your mind so busy covering your tracks, there's no way you can focus on the person you're with. When you're looking for your perfect mate, you must have a clear, quiet mind so you can learn everything about the other person.

When she met Troy at a friend's wedding, Wendy was very self-conscious about her lack of education. Troy had a master's degree in engineering and Wendy felt inferior because she had only a high school diploma and two years of business school. When talking with Troy, she spent a lot of energy controlling the conversation to avoid talking about her educational background. With so much of her energy focused on herself and what she perceived as her shortcomings, she couldn't really enjoy Troy's company. Wendy learned later that, although he had found her attractive, Troy didn't feel completely comfortable with her but couldn't figure out why. The truth is, Wendy was so busy withholding part of herself, it was impossible for Troy to feel any more than a superficial connection.

SHIFT YOUR FOCUS

Life is a grand adventure, but to get the most out of it, you need to lighten up. Every person you meet is unique, and learning about that person is fun. Instead of worrying about what kind of impression you're making, learn to focus on the person you're talking to. Listen carefully to the person and let him or her know you're listening by asking appropriate questions. Trying to impress people often backfires and drives them away. They sense your anxiety and perceive you as desperate. Worst of all, you lose yourself in the process.

On the other hand, when you accept yourself, you come across as happy, confident, and easy to be with and that makes you very desirable. People who are comfortable with themselves draw others to them like a magnet. They're easy to talk to and fun to be around. As you talk with others, ask yourself if you're trying to impress them rather than expressing yourself. You'll know the difference. When you say something to impress someone, you feel uncomfortable. When you say something to express yourself, you feel free and open.

Holly, who was beautiful and always fashionably dressed, couldn't understand why her friend Elizabeth, who was rather plain, easily attracted men. But Elizabeth had a quiet kind of self-confidence that men found very appealing. She was comfortable with herself and felt no need to impress anyone, which made her easy to be with. Elizabeth knew if a man didn't like her for who she was, he wasn't the right man for her. In the meantime, she was having fun meeting all kinds of people.

NO APOLOGY NEEDED

No one is perfect, but we all deserve to be loved even though we have faults. For that to happen, however, we must love ourselves. Don't ever feel you have to apologize for being who you are. Respect yourself, and others will respect you too.

Diana is very verbal and loves to talk and tell long stories. When someone asks her a question, she gives a long and detailed reply. Then she apologizes for talking too much. Diana can't help being verbal, that's just the way she is. It's unnecessary for her to apologize. In fact, it's extremely irritating and prevents her from being taken seriously. Plenty of people are quiet and shy and would love to be around Diana because she'd do the talking for them.

Robin, on the other hand, is always apologizing for being quiet. She is a good listener and enjoys hearing other people's stories or conversations, but is uncomfortable contributing to a discussion herself. Instead of accepting her quiet nature as part of who she is, she turns to the people around her and apologizes for not talking more.

HAVE THE COURAGE OF YOUR CONVICTIONS

Being authentic is also asking for what you want and saying no to what you don't want. If you're out to dinner and want a meal without oil or butter, ask for it. If someone lights a cigarette in your home and you don't want them to, tell them you prefer they smoke outside. Remember, being yourself means standing up for what's important to you. You should be gracious, and sometimes you can compromise, but if you compromise your values or your morality, you've gone too far.

At a college alumni dance, Mia met a man she was really attracted to. She had had a couple glasses of wine earlier in the evening; so when the man offered her another drink, she declined, saying she had to drive home. When he tried to insist, Mia politely but firmly explained she didn't drink if she knew she had to drive. Mia didn't need to seek approval from this man and go against her convictions. She was true to herself.

Like Mia, Stan had the courage of his convictions. At an annual convention for his company, Stan sat at a table with seven other people. As the waitress began serving, Stan, who is a vegetarian, realized he had forgotten to order a vegetarian meal. For a split second, he considered accepting the roast beef being served, just like everyone else at his table. Instead, he stood by his lifestyle choice of the past ten years and asked the waitress if she could find him a vegetarian plate. At first Stan felt the urge to fit in and not make waves but quickly realized it was more important to be true to himself.

ELIMINATE THE NEGATIVE

Now I want to make a shift from the concept of maintaining the integrity of your core beliefs, and explore the subject of personal growth and self-improvement.

With all the modern advances in science, medicine, and therapy there is almost nothing you can't change about yourself. But do you want to? Do you want to change because you want to, or because of some outside influence? Only you know what is the essential and authentic you. Few of us look at ourselves without seeing things we would like to change—things that would not alter our personal authenticity but would make us feel better about ourselves. This is the kind of change and personal growth I encourage.

While you should never compromise your values, there are always areas in life where there's room for improvement. Being comfortable with yourself does not mean being insensitive or tasteless. We all have irritating habits or funny personality quirks. Be honest enough with yourself to admit when a habit is self-destructive or alienating to other people.

Jane met Danny in her bowling league. They had so much fun bowling together each week that when Danny invited her to go with him to a rodeo, Jane accepted. But at the rodeo, Jane was shocked when Danny put a wad of chewing tobacco in his mouth. Every time he spit tobacco juice, she cringed. He did it so frequently, she started counting how many times he spit. When she clocked him spitting eight times a minute, she decided her first date with him would be her last.

Let's face it. There are some habits that aren't socially acceptable no matter how much a part of you you believe they are. Things like belching and spitting are not habits you can expect others to accept. So take stock of your personal habits and, if they would be offensive to most people, get rid of them.

YOU DETERMINE YOUR FUTURE

Even if you're aware of some deep-seated behaviors that have prevented you from finding happiness in past relationships, don't worry. You can change them. We've all been influenced by people and circumstances in our past that affected how we thought, felt, and acted. But I want you to understand one very important point: *your past does not have to determine your future.* It is entirely possible to increase your chances for happiness in a relationship, as well as your self-esteem, by changing your behavior. Regardless of what has happened, you have a *choice* today about how you want to live your life and what type of relationship you want.

Adrienne had a history of unhealthy relationships. She was twenty-eight and had been involved with five men from dysfunctional backgrounds. She knew their backgrounds before getting into the relationships but always thought she could help them in some way. Instead of having a meaningful friendship, she felt like their mother. Whether their problem was drug addiction, depression, or anger, Adrienne tried to fix it. Instead of helping these men, she enabled them. She pampered them, covered up for them, and made excuses for them. In reality, she didn't help them in the least, and worst of all, she hurt herself. She became so enmeshed in their lives that she lost sight of her own needs.

As her fifth relationship ended, Adrienne attended one of my lectures and heard me say your past does not have to determine your future. She made the decision to stop seeing men for awhile in order to spend time by herself to figure out what she liked to do.

For a few weeks, Adrienne read newspapers, magazines, and books to try to figure out what really interested her. She had always liked the theater, but had been so involved with other people's problems she never got the chance to see any shows. She decided to become a season subscriber to a theater in her city. She took a single subscription so she could feel what it was like to have fun by herself.

Adrienne eventually got involved with Mickey, but she approached her new relationship differently. Instead of getting lost in his life, she created healthy boundaries. Adrienne cared about him, but this time she was always aware of her own feelings. She made sure she took care of herself by expressing how she felt and what she wanted. If Mickey had a problem, she listened, but allowed Mickey the freedom to solve his own dilemmas. What started out as Adrienne taking care of herself, ended up as a healthy loving relationship between her and Mickey.

Randy is another person who decided to increase his self-esteem by changing his behavior. Randy had a reputation as a flirt. He had a tendency to enlarge the truth about himself to impress women. For instance, Randy told women he was highly educated and had several advanced degrees. His self-esteem was so low that he spent a lot of his energy covering up who he really was. He worked very hard to hide the fact that he had never finished high school.

Randy was good at finding women who also had low self-esteem. He could tell who they were by how easily they fell for his sweet talk and fabricated stories. Usually women with low self-esteem didn't care whether Randy told the truth or not, they just desperately needed a relationship. Because Randy always dated women who suffered from a poor opinion of themselves, his relationships were destined for failure. It wasn't until Randy was in his seventh unhealthy relationship in one year that he decided to do something to stop attracting unhealthy people. He had purchased my audio cassette program *Light Your Own Fire*, which teaches people how to raise their self-esteem; and after listening to it, he realized that in order to attract someone who had a healthy emotional and mental outlook, he had to have one of his own. Randy decided he didn't want to pretend he had several degrees anymore. He was tired of hiding that he had never graduated from high school, so he decided to get his high school diploma. Once he did that, he felt so good he went to a community college and graduated with a two-year degree in engineering.

While going to school, Randy met Grace who was attracted to him because of his guts and perseverance. She admired his ability to change the course of his life during his midforties, an age when a lot of other people would have given up and settled for where they were in life.

Because Randy did something to boost his self-esteem, he attracted someone who also had a healthy self-concept. Healthy relationships start with healthy people. Randy had a choice in how to handle his low self-esteem. He could have continued to hide the fact he hadn't finished high school and spent the rest of his life lying to women. If he had done that, he would have attracted the kind of women who accept lies in their life—women who think they deserve less than an open, honest relationship.

ACCENTUATE THE POSITIVE

As you work to eliminate your unattractive qualities, don't forget to emphasize attractive ones. Everyone has at least one thing that sets him or her apart. Find it and capitalize on it.

Crystal had perfect teeth, even as a child, and had always received compliments on her beautiful smile; but one day she noticed her smile had lost some of its sparkle. She was well aware that her smile was her best feature and decided to boost her greatest asset by whitening her teeth.

Like Crystal, Bud also learned to capitalize on his best feature. Bud's eyes were a beautiful deep blue and had elicited comments from the time he was a child. As a young man, Bud noticed that he received many compliments when he wore blue; he learned to use his best quality to his advantage by wearing blue frequently.

While we want to emphasize and capitalize on our most attractive physical qualities, it is important to realize that our most meaningful traits lie within. Warmth, compassion, a sense of humor, and unconditional love are far more important than a good figure or perfect teeth. Patricia, for example, is a pleasant-looking woman with regular features whose perfect skin looks great without any makeup, but what attracts most people to her is her warm, compassionate nature. Patricia is one of those people others feel good talking to. It only takes a few minutes before strangers tell Patricia things about themselves they would normally keep secret.

One of your best qualities may be dedication to personal growth. Perhaps you are in counseling for a problem such as drinking or gambling. Even though you may feel vulnerable about it, there's nothing wrong with admitting to someone that you're working on certain aspects of yourself. Granted, you might not want to reveal everything within the first five minutes of meeting someone, but the longer you hide who you really are, the less likely a relationship will survive.

Suppose, for example, you are a smoker who's trying to quit. You meet and are attracted to a nonsmoker, and instead of revealing that you smoke but are working on quitting, you hide it. When the person you are attracted to discovers you smoke, he or she may lose respect for you for concealing it, when that person might have actually admired you for working on quitting if you had been honest at the outset.

SHARE YOURSELF

Most of the time, when you share something about yourself with someone else, you allow that person to feel safe enough to also share something. Again, timing is important. You don't want to tell your life history within the first ten minutes of meeting someone. But once you've developed a rapport and a budding relationship, it's important to gradually share who you really are. That's how trust is formed.

For example, Russ was a recovering alcoholic. When he met Marion he had been sober for two full years, but he couldn't bring himself to mention it. Finally, on their sixth date, shaking and afraid she would want to end their relationship, Russ told Marion the truth. To his surprise and relief, Marion told Russ she had grown up in an alcoholic home where neither of her parents had ever gotten help. Marion was so thrilled to be with someone who was willing to admit the truth and do the work required to stay sober that she embraced Russ warmly and told him how much she respected him. They've now been married fourteen years and have a strong marriage based on love and mutual respect.

DON'T HIDE THE TRUTH

It's natural to want to put your best foot forward when embarking on a new relationship, but hiding a significant fact about yourself can only lead to pain.

Hillary had suffered from chronic migraines all her adult life. After meeting Evan and dating him for a month, she realized he was someone she could spend the rest of her life with, but she was sure he wouldn't want to put up with her regular headaches. She had strategically hidden her migraines from him during the time they had been dating, but for every headache Hillary hid from Evan, she got two more. One night Evan paid Hillary a surprise visit when she was suffering from a migraine. When she opened the door and saw him, Hillary burst into tears. She couldn't hide her condition any longer. She told Evan about her history of headaches, how they impacted her life, and that she had to take medication frequently. When Evan asked her why she had hidden her condition from him, Hillary told him she had been afraid he would think she was weak and inadequate. Evan held her in his arms as he explained that he cared for her and the fact that she suffered from migraines would not affect his feelings. They spent the rest of the evening talking, and between sharing with each other and Evan massaging her temples, Hillary felt a whole lot better by the end of their time together.

NOBODY'S PERFECT

Being imperfect is part of being human. Admitting you have a flaw or a bad habit will often endear you to another person and help him or her feel more comfortable around you.

Amber met Sean on the chairlift at a ski resort. They found they had a lot in common as they talked on the way to the top of the ski run, and they spent the rest of the afternoon skiing together. At the end of the day, Sean asked Amber if she'd like a cup of hot chocolate. She said yes, then realized that if they went inside the ski lodge, she'd have to take off her gloves and reveal her ugly, ragged fingernails.

After sipping hot chocolate and talking for awhile, Sean asked Amber why she still had her gloves on. She considered telling him her hands were still cold, but she really wanted to see him again and knew she wouldn't be able to hide her nails forever. She looked down sheepishly, then told Sean she was embarrassed to admit it, but she was a nailbiter. Sean smiled and told her that it was okay, and confessed that he ground his teeth. He explained that he had to wear a bite plate every night so he wouldn't grind his teeth down to nothing. They both laughed as Amber took off her gloves.

YOU ARE MORE THAN A BODY

Sometimes sharing who you are with someone means you have to get much more personal than talking about nailbiting or teeth-grinding. For example, what if you've had a serious illness that has affected your lifestyle or your appearance?

Many of you already know I was diagnosed with breast cancer in 1991 and underwent a mastectomy and six months of chemotherapy. Then in 1995, I had a recurrence and underwent a bone marrow transplant. As a result of my experiences, I frequently speak to cancer support groups about relationships. I'm often asked, "At what point in a new relationship should I tell the person I have cancer?" My answer is, "When the relationship becomes more than casual." There's a real difference between dumping your personal challenges on someone you've just met, and sharing that you have, or are recovering from, a life-threatening disease with someone you see as a potential partner. Many people are afraid that once they reveal their illness to the person they're dating, that person will no longer want to be with them. In response, I have to ask, "Why would you want to be with someone that insensitive and uncaring?" If someone can't see past your illness or its effects on your body, the person can't see the true you. In my work with these groups, I've heard enough heartwarming stories to know you should never fear sharing the truth with someone you care about.

Hannah and Barry met each other at a mutual friend's Christmas party. After talking for an hour, they felt like they'd known each other all their lives. They began seeing each other several times a week and talking on the phone every night.

Three weeks into their relationship, Barry invited Hannah over to his house for a home-cooked meal. He suggested she bring her bathing suit so she could join him in his new spa.

Hannah accepted Barry's invitation, but was petrified at the thought of wearing her bathing suit. What Barry didn't know was that two years earlier Hannah had had a mastectomy. She hadn't told him about it because she was afraid he wouldn't continue seeing her once he found out she had only one breast.

The night they were to have dinner, Barry picked Hannah up at her house. When Hannah got into his car, Barry could see she was upset about something and asked what was wrong. Hannah burst into tears and told him her history of breast cancer. Barry let her finish her story, then gently wiped away her tears. He looked into Hannah's eyes and told her he cared about her from the inside out, not the outside in, and the fact that she had only one breast didn't affect his feelings for her in the least. They drove to Barry's house and had a wonderful time together. Hannah felt a huge weight had been lifted from her shoulders. How could she not fall in love with someone so caring and sensitive?

Another moving story was told to me by Anthony, who had surgery and treatment for testicular cancer and was left with one testicle. Until he met Emily, he hadn't cared enough about any of the women he dated to share his medical history. Anthony and Emily talked about almost everything; their families, their childhood, and their innermost fears. But Anthony just couldn't bring himself to tell Emily about his surgery. He was embarrassed and afraid she wouldn't want to be with him anymore.

After several months, the anxiety Anthony felt about hiding his surgery from Emily became stronger than his fear of her not wanting to see him anymore, so he decided to tell her. Anthony couldn't believe Emily's reaction. She put her arms around him and told him she felt closer to him than before because of his honesty and vulnerability. What Anthony thought would surely tear their relationship apart, actually strengthened it.

Emily cared about Anthony for who he was: his personality, his interests, his values. The fact that he had one testicle meant nothing to her. She valued Anthony for much more than his body.

We all come with some baggage. No one has a life devoid of secrets, embarrassing habits, or situations that are difficult to share. For example, there are millions of people who have medical conditions that must be discussed with anyone they are seriously considering a relationship with. If you have diabetes, epilepsy, a sexually transmissible disease such as herpes or HIV, or any other condition that impacts your life, it is imperative that you give your potential partner all the information he or she needs to make a fully informed choice about becoming involved with you. Most of the time, the person will be grateful for your honesty and eager to learn more so he or she can support you in your challenge. If you hear the right answer, you'll know this person is someone you want to be in a relationship with. If the person's reaction is negative, it is in your best interests to move on. Remember, you deserve to be loved for who you are and someone out there is worthy of your love.

YOU ARE EXACTLY WHO YOU WERE MEANT TO BE

Like the people in these stories, you are valuable in your own way. You don't have to pretend to be someone you're not or try to make a good impression. You are perfect, just as you are.

It is important for you to feel comfortable with yourself, just as you are. When you can respect and love yourself, you'll attract the perfect person, someone who will love you for your weaknesses as well as your strengths. Although self-improvement is important, you don't ever have to apologize for being you. So live this adventure called life with joy and take pride in knowing you are exactly who you were meant to be!

CHAPTER 1: TAKE ACTION

It's not enough to read how other people have changed their lives. For your life to change, you must take action. At the end of each chapter, there will be assignments to complete, either writing in a journal about your own personal situation, a list of actions to take, or both. Consider the time you spend completing these assignments as an investment in your future, probably the best investment you will ever make.

Get a nice journal, one that makes you feel special, and set aside a time when you will not be disturbed to think about the questions and answers. The journal is for your eyes only, so be completely honest. Although you may have done similar work in the past, complete the work as if you had never thought about these issues before. It's a commitment to yourself that will pay off with the relationship that is perfect for you.

Now, let's get started.

Before you can be yourself, you must know yourself. Use your journal to answer these important questions.

1. Make a list of the core values on which you have built your life and are unwilling to compromise. Your list might include such values as family, religion, health, money, and so on.

2. Your background and life story make you a valuable, worthwhile human being. Under each category, write as much as you can about your personal history.
   - Family
   - Religion/Spiritual Life
   - Neighborhood

- Education
- Health
- Finances

3. When you hide things about yourself, you're not only being dishonest with the other person, you're being dishonest with yourself. In your journal, be honest about the things you'd like to hide. Your list could include physical qualities, habits, opinions, desires, health problems, or anything else you'd be reluctant to have someone else know about you.

4. We all have strengths and weaknesses. Make a list of yours and remember to be honest.

5. It's important to be able to ask for what you want. To help you achieve this, answer the following questions in your journal, then consider what behaviors you may need to work on.
    - If you were a vegetarian and a waitress brought you a meal with meat in it, what would you say?
    - If you didn't allow people to smoke in your car, what would you say to someone who got into your car and lit a cigarette?
    - If you were about to place an order at a delicatessen but someone stepped in front of you, what would you say?
    - If you ordered a rare steak and it was delivered well done, what would you do?

6. Make a list of your personal habits that might be offensive to most people. Then work to eliminate them.

7. Make a list of your attractive qualities. Then circle the ones you want to capitalize on.

8. List the good qualities you possess that may not be evident on the surface. Things such as compassion, empathy, wisdom, generosity, a positive outlook, friendliness, sensitivity, honesty, and courage are the qualities that make us lovable, not our bank balance or our looks.

9. List the things that you're trying to or would like to improve, such as weight, physical condition, vocabulary, learning a foreign language, and so on.

Remember, to find your perfect mate you must give him or her a chance to know who you truly are. Live your life with joy, taking pride in knowing you are exactly who you are meant to be!

With Every Good-Bye
You Learn

SHORT-TERM PAIN, LONG-TERM GAIN

I can't tell you how many people I've talked to who have shut themselves off from having another relationship because they've been hurt in the past. Their fear of being hurt again is so great they refuse to open their hearts to someone new. I know it's painful when a relationship ends, but does that mean you should never open your heart again? Of course not! I'm sure you've heard the expression: It's better to have loved and lost than never to have loved at all. Well, I believe that's true.

No one enjoys being rejected, ignored, disappointed, or pushed aside for a more suitable mate, yet it is these very reactions from the significant people in your life that force you to look inside and ultimately to stretch, grow, and gain more knowledge and understanding about yourself.

Kelly was a young woman who had attended one of my lectures. When I came to the part about self-discovery, she told everyone how the breakup of her two-year relationship with John had contributed to her own self-discovery. When he told her he wanted to see other women, Kelly was completely floored. She couldn't understand it. Kelly told us she had done everything to please John. She had quit college, given up her friends, and stopped participating in a little theater group. As she put it, "I gave up everything for that man!"

Six months after she and John had broken up, Kelly was back in school. She had thought a lot about the ground she lost when she gave up her interests to spend all her time with John. She realized she had become so involved in his life that she had given up her "self." She vowed never to do that again.

In the fall semester she met Paul in one of her night classes. They started dating, but Kelly was so busy with all her activities that he had to wait his turn to see her. Later, he told her she was the most fascinating woman he had ever met. She had so many interests and seemed so happy and content with her life.

Kelly and Paul started seeing each other exclusively, but this time Kelly continued with her activities. Paul didn't mind at all. In fact, he liked her independence and ambition. She knew she was going to be much happier with a man who supported her goals and encouraged her to have outside interests than she ever could have been with a man who demanded all her time and attention. When Paul proposed, Kelly was really glad her experience with John had taught her not to sacrifice her own interests and goals for the sake of a relationship.

Jacob was another person who had to lose a love to learn a lesson. He wrote to tell me he was heartsick he hadn't been aware of my tape programs sooner. He had just finished listening to my *Light Her Fire* tapes, and realized how much he had taken his girlfriend for granted. Even though he now knew exactly how to tell and show her that she was the most important person in his life, he was afraid it was too late since she had broken up with him two weeks earlier. I wrote back that even if it were too late for this relationship, he had learned a valuable lesson if he now knew not to treat his next girlfriend the same way.

About a year later, I received another letter from Jacob, thanking me again for all he had learned. He was engaged to be married to a wonderful woman, who thought he was the most romantic, thoughtful man in the world. He said he had put into practice everything he had learned from my tapes: sending her flowers every few months, giving her small gifts even when there was no special occasion, and sending "I love you cards," often.

The pain of losing someone he cared for motivated Jacob to learn what he could do to improve his next relationship. Without the loss, he would probably have repeated the same mistakes in the future.

LOSE A LOVE, LEARN A LESSON

The breakup of a relationship often brings heartache and pain, but there's a lesson to be learned from the despair, humiliation, and loss you experience. Some lessons are less painful than others, but there is no way we can get through life without learning many lessons along the way.

Some people learn quickly, and only have to make a mistake once to figure out how to correct it. Others may repeat self-defeating behavior several times before they understand its impact, and others have to be hit over the head with a sledgehammer before they see the light.

Jack was one who needed the sledgehammer approach before he would change. Jack owned a computer software business. For years, he had worked twelve hours a day to make the company turn a profit. He promised his wife, Rose, that he would cut back on his hours once the company was on its feet. Four years later, Jack was still working twelve hours a day and seldom spent time with his wife and his two children. One day, Rose told him she had filed for divorce. She was tired of waiting for the company to get on its feet. Jack was shocked and angry that his wife would leave him, especially after he had worked so hard to provide for her and the children.

Three years after Rose and Jack divorced, Jack remarried. His workaholic behavior hadn't changed one bit and his second wife ended up divorcing him for the same reason his first wife had.

After his second divorce, Jack was in a lot of pain. He couldn't understand how yet another woman, whom he had loved very much, could walk out on him. As the pain began to subside, Jack realized if he didn't start enjoying his life outside of work, he was going to spend the rest of his life alone. He learned it didn't matter how much money he made or what his professional title was if he didn't have someone by his side to love and cherish. Jack made a decision to strike a balance between his work and personal life. He delegated some of his responsibilities to other employees and hired an assistant. He used his newfound leisure time to begin enjoying a social life.

Within two years, he met Jane, a single mother with two sons. They fell in love and were married, and Jack is now enjoying his new set of priorities, with his family at the top of the list. They've gone on a family vacation to Hawaii; Jack and Jane take a walk together several times a week; and they've even started taking tennis classes together. After two "good-byes," Jack had finally learned to take time to smell the roses.

Like Jack, Felicia also had a difficult lesson to learn. She and Brad had been married almost seven years when Brad finally had enough. He told Felicia he was sick and tired of trying to please her and walking on eggshells so he wouldn't set off an argument. Brad was a man who did more than most men around the house. He did the grocery shopping and cooked at least three meals a week. He gave their toddler her nightly bath, and he did a lot of the housework as well. He was great about sending Felicia flowers, he called her a couple of times each day to see how she was doing, and was always willing to do whatever Felicia asked of him. Still, Felicia found things to complain about. Brad felt like nothing he did was ever right. He had no idea what it would take to please this woman and he decided to quit trying. He and Felicia split up.

With Brad gone, Felicia had to take care of everything, and realized what a gem he had been. She really missed his help and loving ways, and, little by little, began to understand how ungrateful and demanding she had been. Although she had destroyed any chance for love in their relationship, Felicia still felt she owed Brad an apology. She told him she was sorry for the way she had treated him and hoped some-day he'd have someone in his life who would treat him as well as he deserved.

One night Felicia saw my infomercial and ordered my tape program, *Light His Fire*. She listened to it whenever she had a chance and gradually the lessons began to sink in. Felicia learned to see and be grateful for the blessings in her everyday life and when she met and fell in love with Clint a few years after her divorce, she promised herself she would pay him a compliment every day and always notice what he did right.

WAKE-UP CALLS

The end of a relationship is a wake-up call that can take you to deeper levels of intimacy and commitment in your next relationship. By looking at past relationships and examining their lessons, we can become better partners in the future.

When his first marriage ended in divorce, Joe blamed his former wife. He was very angry that after fourteen years of marriage, she decided to leave without even talking about it. For the next several years, he stayed stuck on his ex-wife's self-ishness, lack of commitment, and unwillingness to communi-cate. He was so focused on what she did wrong, that he never stopped to see what his responsibility might have been. He finally began to look at his own part in the marital breakup and realized he had been coasting since their first anniversary.

In reality, Joe's wife had made many attempts at commu-nication, but Joe had been so wrapped up in watching sports on TV that he had completely tuned her out. Joe was a seri-ous sports fan who felt deprived if he missed a televised sports event. The only sports his wife enjoyed watching were ice skating and the Winter Olympics.

After their divorce, Joe could watch TV to his heart's content. He didn't have to be annoyed by his wife's interruptions or feel guilty anymore. But a strange thing happened. Joe was lonely. He missed his wife and found that watching TV left him feeling empty.

Little by little, he became a participant instead of a spectator. He took up golf, joined a bowling league, and even played some basketball on the weekends. He met his future wife while bowling. She was on the same team and they had a great time together, "high-fiving" when one of them scored a strike and congratulating each other whenever one of them bowled particularly well. When they started dating, Joe talked to Karen about his marriage. When she asked what went wrong, he said he was just beginning to understand. He explained that he had been more interested in watching TV than in nurturing his relationship. He added that he had a whole new lease on life now and TV was a very small part of it. Before they got married, Joe promised Karen to love, honor, and listen, and vowed she would never have to compete with their television for equal time. Joe's divorce was the wake-up call he needed to make him a better partner in his next relationship.

Christine's wake-up call also came in the form of divorce. The day Christine's husband, David, told her he wanted a divorce was probably the worst day of her life. She had no idea David would do something like that. They had been married for more than ten years and had three children. Even though there had been no passion in their marriage for the last eight years,

David was a great father and Christine never dreamed he would leave. Christine wanted to know, "What's so wrong with our marriage you'd be willing to leave me and the children?"

David explained to Christine that he was still a young man and needed more than his children to fulfill himself. David said he wanted some love and passion in his life, not just a casserole on the table and someone to care for the children while he was at work. "I could pay someone to do those things," he said. "I need a companion, a partner, a lover. You haven't even tried to be those things to me. I can't live like this anymore."

When he moved out, David did everything he could to make it easier for Christine and the children. He found a house just a few blocks away so that the children could come over anytime and feel as comfortable in his house as they did in their own home. And he still mowed Christine's lawn every weekend and did other chores around the house to keep it looking good.

Christine missed David very much. She realized what a wonderful husband she had lost and really searched her heart to understand what had gone wrong. When her best friend told her about my *Light His Fire* tapes, Christine listened to them and came to understand that once the children had come along, she had focused all her attention on them and stopped being a mate to her husband. She had neglected her appearance, making no effort to keep herself looking attractive to her husband, had ignored his sexual needs, and had even ignored his emotional needs. She decided that if she were ever given another opportunity for a relationship, she would cherish her husband in a whole new way.

A few years after her divorce, Christine met Jim, who was a loan officer at the bank where she worked. They fell in love and were married a year and a half after they met. Christine remembered everything she had learned, and Jim says he's the luckiest man in the world to have a wife who is so attentive to his needs and so available to him, while still being a good mother to all five of their children (her three and his two).

NO RELATIONSHIP IS A WASTE OF TIME

Being in a relationship is our greatest opportunity to learn and grow. It gives us a chance to discover things about ourselves that we might not have known otherwise. Being in a difficult relationship is often the catalyst that wakes us up to our weaknesses and motivates us to change.

Chad and Rebecca had been dating exclusively for a short time when jealousy reared its ugly head. Every day Chad gave Rebecca the third degree. In his words: "I was like a drill sergeant, and I treated Rebecca like a new recruit. I questioned her about where she'd been, who she'd seen, what they had talked about. And when she answered, I'd say things like, 'Yeah, sure. Tell me the truth.'" If Chad saw Rebecca talking to another man, he'd accuse her of flirting. His jealousy got so bad that he even began to follow her around. Rebecca told Chad that she might as well cheat on him, since he was so convinced that was what she was doing. It wasn't long before Rebecca told Chad she couldn't stand his possessiveness and jealousy, and she broke up with him.

Chad knew his jealousy was out of control. He really regretted all the crazy things he'd done in the relationship and knew he needed some answers. He went to the library and got some self-help books and learned all he could about jealousy. He concluded that his lack of trust had nothing to do with who he was with but was based on his own lack of self-esteem. He worked on replacing his negative thoughts about himself with positive ones, and, by the time he became involved in another relationship, he was able to feel deserving of the love his new girlfriend showed him. He trusted her love for him and knew he had no reason to doubt her.

ONE DOOR CLOSES, ANOTHER DOOR OPENS

Just because you've had an unfortunate experience in one relationship is no reason to suppose you can't be happy in another one. Many people have lost a love, only to find another greater than the one they lost.

Alice and Norman had been married for three years when they decided to start a family. After trying unsuccessfully to become pregnant for over a year, Alice discovered she needed a hysterectomy. They were both crushed by the knowledge that Alice could never have a child, and the next few years were spent exploring other options. When all was said and done, Norman was not open to any of them. He absolutely insisted he had to have children of his own. After much soul-searching, Norman divorced Alice.

Alice was absolutely shattered by Norman's decision. Not only had she lost all hope of having children, she had lost a husband she loved. Alice felt her life was over. Then one day, when she was standing in line at the supermarket, she met Desmond. He had so many groceries that he actually had two carts to empty. Alice started helping Desmond put his groceries on the conveyor belt and asked if he was shopping for an army or was just hungry. "I've always heard it's not a good idea to go shopping if you haven't eaten all day," she joked. Desmond told Alice he was a widower with three children. He had two daughters, a ten-year-old and a six-year-old, and a son who was fourteen and ate as much as two full-grown adults.

Alice and Desmond chatted so easily that they found it hard to end their conversation. Before leaving, Desmond mentioned that he shopped every Friday evening on his way home from work. The next Friday, Alice made sure she was in the store at the same time as the previous week. She looked for Desmond and was about to conclude she had missed him when she saw him come around the end of the pet food aisle. When he stopped in front of the dog food, Alice approached him and said, "Don't tell me you have a dog, too." Desmond's eyes lit up in recognition. They talked for a while and soon Desmond suggested they meet somewhere for breakfast the next morning. Alice agreed and it wasn't long before she was invited to meet Desmond's three children and two dogs. Alice fell in love with all of them in a heartbeat, and when she and Desmond were married in the backyard, even the dogs were in attendance. When her marriage to Norman ended, Alice thought her life had ended too. In reality, it had just begun. If Norman hadn't left her, Alice would never have had the wonderful family she acquired when she married Desmond.

When he lost his wife of thirty-three years, Fred also learned that when one door closes, another door opens. Jeanette had been almost totally paralyzed by a stroke right after their thirtieth anniversary. They had just returned from an Alaskan cruise the week before when she collapsed as she was folding the laundry. Jeanette needed full-time care, and rather than putting her in a nursing home, Fred hired a live-in nurse.

Gradually, Fred and the nurse, Willa, became close friends. In the evenings, after Jeanette was settled and sleeping, they would sit in the den with a cup of tea. Over the next few months, they came to know each other's hopes, fears, and life stories. When Fred's children came to visit their mother, they always spent some time chatting with Willa; and Willa, who had no children, adopted Fred's family as her own.

Jeanette's condition worsened over time, and she didn't survive her second stroke. Fred had been a devoted husband who took on the responsibility of Jeanette's care on the weekends when Willa was off-duty. When Jeanette died, he was at a complete loss. Even though her illness had been devastating and he knew her death was a blessing, he missed her terribly. Not only had he lost Jeanette, he had also lost his friend Willa, who took another job when she was no longer needed at Fred's home.

One evening, he called Willa at her new place of employment and asked if she would have dinner with him on her next day off. She agreed, and when they met, it felt as if they had come home again. They started seeing each other on weekends, and after a year or so, Fred asked Willa to marry him. She accepted and they will be celebrating their tenth anniversary this year.

When his wife died, Fred had no idea he could ever be happy with another woman. He blessed the day he hired Willa to be Jeanette's nurse, not only because she took such good care of his wife, but because she became an important person in his life.

A BLESSING IN DISGUISE

Often when things don't work out the way we had hoped, there's a reason that eludes us at the time, but which becomes clear somewhere down the road.

When Lana, a committed marathon runner, suffered a crippling injury she was brokenhearted. She had spent hours every week training, and she had loved the feeling she got whenever she could cut her time by even a few seconds. She had entered the New York Marathon and was looking forward to finishing with the front runners, when she fell during a training run and injured her leg very badly. Her leg was put in a cast and Lana was told it would take at least a year for her leg to heal enough to start training again. In the meantime, she would need physical therapy to strengthen her torn ligaments once her cast was off.

Lana found it very hard being incapacitated. She lived in New York City and used public transportation to get around. With her leg in a cast, she had a hard time going anywhere. Fortunately, her employer provided a car and driver to take her to and from work, but she was confined to her apartment for much of the time she wasn't at work. One day, dreading another weekend in her apartment alone, Lana called a friend, Don, who lived in Cleveland

and asked if she could go visit for the weekend. Her friend was delighted, and offered to pick Lana up at the airport. He warned her, though, that his college roommate was also visiting for the weekend and told Lana if she wanted to wait until another time that would be fine too. Lana couldn't bear the thought of staying in New York, so she decided to visit Don anyway.

It was the best decision Lana ever made. When Don picked her up at the airport, Lana couldn't believe her eyes. Standing next to him at the gate was the best-looking man she had ever seen. Her heart beat wildly as she realized she was going to get to spend the weekend with this man. She only hoped he was as interesting as he was handsome.

Don, Lana, and Lee had a wonderful weekend together. Lee was even more than Lana had hoped for. He was funny, considerate, and charming. By the time she boarded her plane to return home, Lana knew that fate had kicked in when she fell and injured her leg. If she hadn't hurt herself, she never would have met Lee and she thanked God for the accident that brought her to her future husband.

Judith, whom I met at one of my courses, experienced an emotional blow that left her feeling crippled, when her husband told her he didn't want to be with her anymore. Judith and Sam had been married for seven years, and Judith knew they had a problem. She didn't enjoy sex with Sam and felt as if there were something wrong with her. She talked to her best friend about it, but when her best friend suggested that maybe Sam just wasn't the person that could ring Judith's bell, she rejected the idea. "I'm sure it's not Sam's fault. He says I must be frigid," Judith said.

Eventually, Sam asked Judith for a divorce, saying she was cold. He wanted a passionate woman, one who would respond to him with fire, one who desired him as much as he desired her. Judith couldn't blame Sam for feeling that way, and although she still loved him, she had to let him go.

For a long time, Judith was afraid to get involved with another man. She felt defective and didn't imagine she had anything to offer. However, when she met Tyler her attraction to him was too strong to resist. She loved the way he looked, she loved the way he talked, she loved the way he smiled, she loved everything about him. Tyler felt the same way about Judith. He was always touching her lovingly. He stroked her hair, touched her lightly on the shoulder or arm, put his hand on the small of her back as they walked. When they danced together, their bodies fit together like they were meant for each other. Judith felt a desire for Tyler that she had never felt with Sam.

When they got married, Judith discovered that she was a normal woman, in fact, a passionate woman, who had no trouble responding to this man she loved so much. Judith realized that Sam hadn't really made love to her at all. He had simply used her. He had never talked to Judith about his feelings of love for her, the way Tyler did. The only time he had touched her was during sex. He had never touched her during the day the way Tyler did. Judith realized that she and Sam had never actually shared any kind of real intimacy. What she had thought was missing in her, was in reality something missing in Sam. Judith was so grateful that she and Sam had not stayed together. If they had, she never would have known the kind of love she experienced with Tyler.

TEACHERS ALONG THE WAY

Many times when someone breaks up with another person, he or she isn't honest about the reason. Rather than hurt someone's feelings, the person may say something like: It's not you. It's me; I'm falling out of love, I don't know why; there just isn't any chemistry between us; I just don't have time to be involved in a relationship right now; I'm just not ready to get serious; or, I need to concentrate on my job right now.

These kinds of vague excuses may lessen the painful impact, but they don't give you any insight into your own role in the breakup. While it may be painful to hear, when someone tells you the truth, he or she is really doing you a favor. Instead of being defensive, open your heart to what you are being told and thank the person for his or her kindness. It's very rare for someone to care enough to tell the truth about why a relationship is over.

Nadine and Scott had dated for almost a year. About six months after they started dating, Nadine noticed that Scott was making almost all the decisions in their relationship. If Nadine made a suggestion, Scott listened politely and then rationalized doing it his way. Whether it was which movie to see or how much to spend at a restaurant, Scott always had to have his way.

Nadine tried to talk to Scott about his controlling nature, but he wouldn't listen. Finally, Nadine told Scott she wanted to date other people. He was very hurt and angry.

After they stopped seeing each other, Scott vowed he was through with dating and closed himself off from women. After several months, he became tired of the loneliness and pain he had been feeling. He started to think about all the things

Nadine had said about him. He began to wonder if what she had said was true. Maybe he had been too opinionated. Maybe he was too controlling. He slowly started to date again. Only this time, he was aware how important it was to compromise with whomever he went out with. Little by little, Scott learned to listen to his date's suggestions and even follow them. He realized he didn't always have to be the one with the answers.

Even though Scott suffered when his relationship with her ended, Nadine turned out to be a wonderful teacher for him. Because of her reaction to his behavior, Scott is now in an easy, rewarding relationship full of love and compromise.

Eve and Frank had been married for five years, and Frank was quickly getting disenchanted. They had no life together. Eve was a partner in a high-powered law firm, and she worked, 60, 70, even 80 hours a week. Frank was a general contractor, who went to bed early and left the house by 4:30 every morning. He was usually home by 4:30 in the afternoon, and he rarely had to work weekends. Eve, on the other hand, was at work every night until at least 8 or 9 o'clock, worked every single Saturday, and many Sundays as well. The only time Frank got to see Eve was when he met her for dinner near her office and they had a quick meal together before she returned to work.

Frank asked Eve to slow down. He told her he missed her and wanted to spend some quality time with her, but Eve replied that she couldn't slow down. "If I don't pull my weight at the firm, I'll lose my credibility and my partnership. I've worked too hard for this to just let it go." Frank tried to entice Eve with a cruise to the Caribbean, but Eve wouldn't budge. "I can't take the time, Frank," she said. "That's all there is to it. Why don't you go alone? We'll take a vacation together next year."

Frank sighed and changed the subject, but later when he thought about it he remembered Eve's suggestion that he take a vacation alone. Why not, he thought. I might as well have some fun in life, even if it is alone. He booked his cruise and told Eve his plans. She barely responded to his announcement and was too busy to take him to the airport the day he left to start his vacation.

When Frank returned home from his cruise, he told Eve he wanted a divorce. She was shocked when he told her he had met a woman on the cruise and he thought he was in love with her. Eve had been so busy with her work, that she hadn't even realized how truly unhappy and lonely Frank had been. She tried to change his mind, promising she would change, but Frank wasn't swayed. He wanted out.

When Frank left, Eve went to pieces. She couldn't concentrate, she'd lost her drive, and her work began to suffer. She decided to take some time off to try and get herself together. She took long walks in the park, watched the sun set over the ocean, read books and listened to tapes, and got enough sleep for the first time in years. During her time off she came to realize that her drive for success had not only robbed her husband of a wife, it had robbed her of a life. She made the decision to give up her partnership in the law firm, and go back to being a corporate lawyer for a company she had worked for on her way up the career ladder. Somehow, taking that step backwards didn't seem like the end of the world any more. In fact, it seemed like it was a step in the right direction, the first one she'd made in many years.

When she took her new position, Eve made it clear to her employer she had a personal life that was very important to her and she wouldn't be working the kind of hours she had worked before. She was very happy with her new lifestyle, and it showed on her face. She smiled more, she laughed more, and she took an interest in the people around her. Eventually she met Conrad, an executive in the company where she worked, and they began to date. When they were married, Eve and Conrad took a very long honeymoon trip to the South Pacific, something Eve had never considered possible when she had been a hard-driven partner of a law firm.

SILENCE IS GOLDEN

The end of a relationship is often accompanied by turmoil. You may feel angry, guilty, or vengeful. To learn the lesson that's in store for you, you must be able to silence your mind. Until we can quiet our thoughts, we can't listen carefully for the lesson.

Men and women in prison have become enlightened and understood the error of their ways because they were forced to be alone with themselves. If you take away all the distractions of the outside world, you can't help but look within yourself. Obviously you don't need a prison cell to quiet your mind, but you do need to give yourself the time, and the peace and quiet to be able to learn the lesson the breakup of your relationship holds for you.

Noah was very hopeful when Daisy accepted his invitation for their fifth date. He couldn't remember the last time he had dated someone for this length of time. Usually, women stopped accepting his invitations after the second or third date.

Noah's hope turned to despair when, at the end of his fifth date with her, Daisy told him she didn't want to go out with him again. Unlike all the other women he had dated, Daisy told Noah why she didn't want to date him anymore. In a nice but firm way, she told him she thought he was self-centered. She gave him several examples of how his self-centeredness manifested itself, the biggest one being that he talked about himself most of the time. She told him she wanted to be with someone who cared about what she had to say.

After Daisy ended their relationship, Noah found as many people as he could who would agree with him that he wasn't the one with the problem. He worked very hard to build a case against Daisy, so that he wouldn't have to look within himself. But even after talking to lots of people, Noah still didn't feel good. It wasn't until he spent some time alone in his apartment and really thought about what Daisy had said that he could admit that what she told him was true. He realized that he was self-absorbed. As hard as it was to face, Noah learned a great lesson from the pain he felt from Daisy's words. His pain was what made his next relationship a successful one.

HONOR THY RELATIONSHIP

Sometimes a relationship ends for no apparent reason. Both partners were good people. He was reliable, steady, dependable. She was hard-working, faithful, fastidious. What went wrong?

Often, the best way to understand what went wrong in a relationship, is to understand why you got together in the first place. Did you become involved in this relationship on the rebound? Were you lonely and trying to fill a void? Were you tired of being single when all of your friends were married? Was your home life with your parents so painful that you were willing to accept any port in a storm? Were you looking for stability after years of upheaval and uncertainty? Was your physical attraction so strong you were unable to see what kind of person you were getting involved with?

Asking yourself these questions will help you look at your past relationships from a different perspective. Instead of focusing on the pain that ensued as the relationship fell apart, you can begin to understand that it was probably doomed from the beginning, and as a result you will be better able to choose the right mate for yourself in the future.

The thing to remember is that every relationship is worthy. When your relationship ends, honor it for the good it has brought to your life. There is something positive to be gained from every experience in life, even from a relationship that causes you pain and suffering. Your beautiful children, your increased awareness of yourself, the people you met and became close to as a result of your relationship, the new ideas you were exposed to, the skills you learned, the fun you had (admit it, you had some fun) are all reasons to be grateful. If you've had a relationship that has ended, bless it for the good it has brought to you and prepare to move on to the relationship of your dreams with your perfect mate.

CHAPTER 2: TAKE ACTION

Life is full of lessons. Even if you've never been in a relationship, you've had other painful experiences in life. The following exercises will help you to understand the lessons those experiences held for you.

Using your journal:

1. Reflect on a past relationship or painful experience and write a paragraph describing what was most painful about it.

2. Thinking about that same relationship or experience, describe a positive lesson you learned from it.

3. Again, using that same relationship or experience, describe how it benefited you.

4. Describe how the knowledge you gained from your past relationship will help you in the future.

Your past relationships have prepared you for a future full of promise. Be grateful for what you have learned, knowing that your lessons have made you a better partner and have given you the knowledge you need to make better choices as you conduct your search for your perfect mate.

Let's Get Personal

Knowing yourself, learning from past relationships, and believing that you deserve to be happy are certainly critical steps in achieving the relationship of your dreams, but how do you go about finding the perfect partner for you?

As I emphasized in the introduction to this book, you must take action. There are hundreds of ways to meet people, but to maximize your chances you have to try many different ways, rather than relying on those that occur naturally during the course of your life. Although many people have met their mate at work or through friends, you wouldn't be reading this book if meeting potential partners was something that happened for you on a regular basis.

In this chapter, I'm going to tell you about one of the fastest, easiest, and least expensive ways I know of to meet people—one that is guaranteed to provide dozens of men or women eager to meet you. Can you imagine how much fun it would be to come home from work every day to find multiple messages on your answering machine asking for a return call and a chance to get to know you? That's exactly what can happen, if you'll just muster up a little trust and the willingness to have some fun.

Let me tell you a story. Years ago, in the early days of my Light His Fire class, I learned a lesson from two of my students that benefited countless people over the years. Caroline and Katherine, single women who were interested in finding relationships, weren't meeting any men. They put their heads together and decided to chip in on a shared personal ad in a local paper. Although they were nervous, they figured they had nothing to lose and everything to gain. Even if the ad led nowhere, they reasoned, they would have fun in the process. This is the ad they placed:

TWO FOR ONE

Two women, ages 35 and 45, have never advertised before. Looking for moonlight walks on the beach, romantic candlelight dinners, possible long-term relationship.

They received over one hundred responses, went out with about twenty-five men each and both fell in love and married. That was when I first realized that a personal ad was an incredible way for my students to meet the man or woman of their dreams. Since then, placing a personal ad has been part of the homework assignment in all of my classes.

I know you're probably thinking that this has got to be the worst idea you've ever heard, but before you roll your eyes and shake your head in protest, hear me out. I'm used to getting a negative reaction when I introduce this subject in my classes, but I think I can convince you, just as I did my students, that a personal ad really is a great idea.

For example, Sue, a woman in one of my classes, was recently divorced and was not interested in a relationship at this point in her life. In fact, the only reason she was taking my class was because a friend, who wanted to bring back the passion in her marriage, roped her into it. When I gave the personal ad homework assignment, Sue rejected the idea. But after she saw the responses the other students received, she decided to try it just for fun. At our fourth class meeting, she reported that she had gotten responses from forty different men and was about to go on her second date with one of them. The night of the last class Sue was accompanied by her new beau. A year later, Sue and Al were married and not long after that I received a note saying that they were expecting their first child. Now, that's what I call results!

Another student, a single man in one of my Light Her Fire classes, looked at me as if I were crazy when I brought up the topic of personal ads. I just smiled at him and said, "Look, you have nothing to lose. Place the ad and if you don't like the responses you get, don't call anyone back." Because he had paid to take my class and he wanted to get his money's worth, he finally agreed. Reluctantly, he put together an ad that displayed his sense of humor. I don't remember exactly what he wrote, but I do remember he said something like this:

OPEN WIDE

Dentist, 45, looking for a woman who can maintain her end of a conversation so I won't feel like I'm pulling teeth!

Our dentist met a delightful woman, a teacher, who was a great conversationalist. They were head-over-heels in love with each other by the time he graduated from my six-week class.

One of my readers met her future husband through the personals as well. Joyce, a 46-year-old insurance agent, was the divorced mother of two daughters. Joyce sent me a letter and a newspaper article which described how she and her fiancé met through a personal ad in that same paper. The ad she had responded to went something like this:

THE EYES HAVE IT

42-year-old divorced-white-male, big brown eyes, 6 feet, 175 pounds, non-smoker, enjoys romantic movies, children, shopping and dining. Total communication. Looking for white female 36–46, slender to medium, for long-term relationship/commitment.

Joyce called and left a message. When Jim called her back, Joyce learned that he was a heavy equipment mechanic and that he, too, had a daughter. After talking awhile, Jim asked if Joyce would like to go for coffee. The coffee date went well and led to a dinner date. Six months later, Jim sent Joyce on a love hunt, which he had learned about from reading my book, *Light Her Fire*. The love hunt eventually led Joyce to one of the finest restaurants in the city, where Jim surprised her with a diamond ring and a proposal of marriage. She was writing to thank me for the insight Jim had gained by reading my book. In her letter Joyce said, "When Jim shared your book with me, I realized how much your creative wisdom had influenced him. I'm looking forward to many years of marriage with this man who is so sensitive and aware of my every emotion."

Every major newspaper has a section devoted to personal ads. Even if you never place or respond to one yourself, just seeing the number of ads placed by both men and women who are seeking a relationship makes you realize that it's not true when people say, "There's no one out there," or "All the good ones are taken." You can call any major newspaper in the country and they will confirm that people from all walks of life place and answer personal ads. Lawyers, doctors, accountants and other professionals, even models—men and women whose looks are their stock in trade—are looking for a mate in the personals column. I once had the opportunity to interview a male model. When I asked him why he had placed a personal ad he said, "When I go to photo shoots I see a lot of beautiful women, but we're all there to work. There's really no time to get to know anyone."

Many people have very busy lives and don't have the time or the opportunity to meet people. In addition, there are many reasons people don't want to date someone they meet on the job. For one, if they started dating and it didn't work out, they might feel awkward seeing each other at work every day. For another, some companies have a policy prohibiting members of the same family working together. So, if two people from the same company started dating and then married, one of them would have to leave his or her job. Sexual harassment laws have also impacted dating in the workplace.

In this world of rush, rush, rush and work, work, work, a personal ad is a wonderful way to meet that special someone. With a personal ad, you can meet more people in a few weeks than you could meet in an entire year of attending parties or single's events. In the last chapter of this book, I talk about fifty-one ways to meet your perfect mate. I believe you will meet someone by employing each and every one of those ways . . . eventually. But if you want to meet a lot of people in a short time, placing a personal ad is the way to do it!

Nicole spent three years searching for a compatible mate by frequenting singles dances, going on blind dates, and attending friends' parties. During those three years, she had a lot of fun and dated many people, but she never met anyone with whom she wanted to pursue a serious relationship. While taking my class, Nicole gathered up the courage to place a personal ad in her city newspaper. She told me later that she dated more men during the six months she ran the ad than she had during the three years she spent trying to meet people through friends and singles events.

I strongly encourage you to continue meeting people by using the fifty-one ways I describe in the last chapter, but if you are eager to meet someone quickly, a personal ad will insure that you meet lots of people in the shortest time possible.

OVERCOMING NEGATIVITY

I know that the idea of placing a personal ad will be met with strong resistance by many of you. Perhaps you find the idea embarrassing or worry that you'll be labeled as weird or a loser by your friends or that they will think you're desperate and grasping at anything to keep from spending the rest of your life alone. Nothing could be further from the truth. Yes, you are looking for someone to share your life with, but placing a personal ad puts you in the driver's seat. You write the ad. You decide who to go out with, and you decide who you want to continue a relationship with. That's not being a loser, that's being a winner.

Some readers, especially women, may be concerned about the safety of meeting someone in this way, but I wouldn't suggest it if I felt it were too risky. Because you have a chance to get acquainted over the phone before you ever meet in person, I believe a personal ad is much safer than meeting someone in a bar who might offer to pick you up for your first date. Anytime you begin dating someone new, you are taking a risk. There are no guarantees, whether you meet through a mutual friend, at a bar, or through a personal ad. To minimize the risk, I always advise people to arrange the first meeting in a busy public place, such as a popular coffee shop. Meet during daylight hours if possible and always have your own transportation to and from your meeting place. Let common sense and your intuition guide you and in all likelihood, the worst thing you'll experience will be a bad case of coffee nerves from all those coffee dates.

Jenny, one of my students, met her husband of ten years through a personal ad. When other women in the class expressed their fear of meeting someone in that way, Jenny shared that she had felt completely comfortable when she finally met John because they had spent three phone calls getting to know each other before they even set a date to meet. That's what's so great about the personals. They allow you the luxury of not having to give the other person your address or phone number until you are sure he or she is the type of person you would like to meet.

A GREAT TIMESAVER

Another positive aspect of using a personal ad is that you get to state the qualities you do or don't want in a mate. I can't think of a better way for you to know if a candidate is potentially a good match than by running a personal ad. When you meet someone in a social situation you can't say, "I'm not interested. You smoke and I don't," "You have children and I don't want any," "You're too tall, I'd like someone shorter," or "I'm religious, you're not." Usually, when you meet someone at a party or a singles event, you can't really qualify that person until after several dates. Although you may have had a pleasant time with the person, you come to realize that he or she has certain qualities you don't want in a lifelong partner. By then, several weeks may have gone by and you're no closer to finding your perfect mate than you were before. On the other hand, when writing a personal ad, the sky's the limit. This is your chance to define your ideal mate and then advertise for him or her.

Sid met Gloria at a friend's company Christmas party. He was initially attracted to her because of her smile. She wasn't too tall and she had red hair, two things he especially liked in a woman. At first glance, Gloria appeared to be someone he would be interested in getting to know.

They spent two hours talking about their professions and their educational backgrounds. When Sid found out that

Gloria had a graduate degree, he was thrilled. Meeting some-one who enjoyed learning was very important to him.

They went on several dates during the next few weeks and really enjoyed being with each other. It wasn't until their fifth date that Sid learned that Gloria didn't believe in God. He was stunned. They hadn't talked about religion or spirituality until then, and Sid couldn't believe what he was hearing. Although Sid didn't attend church regularly, he had a very strong faith.

Gloria and Sid spent the next two dates trying to under-stand each other's personal beliefs. But no matter how they tried, neither could accept the position of the other. They agreed to stop seeing each other and move on in their search for a mate.

It was Sid's experience with Gloria that finally convinced him to place a personal ad. He didn't regret meeting Gloria. He'd had fun and had enjoyed all of their interesting discus-sions, but he was tired of putting in weeks of his time dating someone only to find out that they weren't compatible in basic areas.

Once Sid started placing ads, he couldn't believe he hadn't done it before. It was so easy, and the best part was he knew something about his dates before he even met them! He learned to screen people by making his ad specific enough to attract women in his age group, at the postgrad-uate level, and who had a strong faith in God.

Imagine how exciting it was for Sid to come home, pick up the phone, dial his personal code, and hear a voice on the other end that was responding to his ad! He said it gave him something to look forward to every single day.

Some people like to place ads, some prefer to respond to ads, and some like to do both. Just keep in mind that if you place the ad, you're in control. You'll be receiving all the calls and you'll get to decide which ones to respond to. However, if you see something you can't resist, by all means, make the call. Be aware, though, that you may be the fiftieth caller and the person who placed the ad is busy responding to callers two or three and can't possibly get to you. Although it's discouraging not to receive a return call, don't take it personally.

ONE STEP AT A TIME

The best way to tackle a big project is to break it down into smaller steps. Let's begin the project of placing your personal ad by taking baby steps. First, I want you to ask yourself why you're placing this ad. My guess is you'll answer, "To meet someone!" Although you may very well meet your perfect mate by placing a personal ad, for now I want you to let go of the outcome. Just think of it as a grand adventure, an opportunity to have fun and meet people from all different walks of life. Stephanie, another of my students, still talks about how she dated a fireman, a high school math teacher, a beekeeper, and a ski instructor all in the same month. Like Stephanie, just plan to have a good time and enjoy the process!

To begin, I'd suggest that you visit a newsstand and buy copies of all the local newspapers. Check out the costs of personal ads and find out what the circulation is. Besides newspapers, there are publications targeted specifically at different types of people: singles, senior citizens, hobbyists, professionals, and so on. You might also want to buy any magazines that pertain to the type of person you wish to meet and that carry personal ads.

Start by reading ads other people have written. Circle the ones you like and think about how you might improve or combine a few of them to make an ad that suits you. Try writing some ads of your own. Don't worry about your ad being too wordy at this point, just have fun seeing what you come up with. Keep playing with your practice ad until it feels right for you. Trust your instincts. You know better than anyone what you want in a mate.

After you've had some fun playing with your practice ads, it's time to get serious. Before you write your real ad, you need to spend some time thinking about who you are. It's important to understand you are unique and special and deserve to find someone who loves and appreciates you as you really are. In past relationships you may have tried so hard to please your partner that you lost the real you. If so, this is your chance to start with a clean slate. What is it that you love to do? Where would you love to go? What are your values, your goals, your aspirations? What really matters to you?

Although you may think you know everything there is to know about yourself, it's very important to take a written inventory at this time. Remember, this is a brainstorming session, so don't limit yourself. Write down as many things as you can think of that apply to you. Even though you won't use everything you've written here in your ad, you can refer to this information later, when you are talking on the phone with people who respond to your ad.

To get you started, let's look at ten different categories for you to think about. As you complete each category, keep in mind that there are no right or wrong answers, only answers that describe you.

In your journal, answer the following questions.

WHO AM I?

1. *Personality*

   Do you have a good sense of humor? Are you shy or out-going? Are you a good talker or a good listener or maybe both? Are you a risk taker? Anything that describes your personality would go under this category.

2. *Hobbies*

   What do you enjoy doing when you're not working? Maybe you like to read, play an instrument, or paint. Do you like to watch old movies or listen to classical music? Do you go to garage sales, flea markets, or swap meets? Do you enjoy board games like Scrabble, Monopoly, or Pictionary?

3. *Family*

   Do you come from a large or a small family? Do you have children? Do you want children someday?

4. *Physical Traits*

   Do you have blue eyes, brown eyes, green eyes? What is your hair color? If you're a man, are you bald or losing your hair? (Don't worry if you are. Plenty of women find it makes a man look distinguished, exotic, or sexy.)

5. *Travel*

   Where have you been and where do you want to go? Do you enjoy camping and sleeping under the stars? Do you dream of backpacking your way through Europe? Maybe you only like hotels or bed and breakfast inns. Is sailing or cruising your dream vacation?

6. *Religion*

   Are you a religious person? Do you practice traditions that go along with your religion? Is it an important part of your life?

7. *Sports*

   Do you like football, basketball, baseball, or soccer? Are you a spectator or a participant? Do you play golf or tennis?

8. *Health Habits*

   Do you drink or smoke? Are you into health food or junk food? Maybe you're a vegetarian.

9. *Exercise*

   Do you keep in shape or not? If you do, what's your favorite form of exercise? Do you like to dance? Are you a weight lifter? A runner? Maybe you enjoy yoga or rollerblading.

10. *Politics*

    Do you feel strongly about political issues? Are you a democrat, republican or independent?

WHO IS MY PERFECT MATE?

Once you have a really clear picture of "wonderful you," it's time to think about the wonderful person who's going to come into your life. Imagine your fairy godmother is standing in front of you, asking you to describe your perfect mate. What traits would he or she have? Use the same list as before, only this time describe the traits you desire in your perfect mate. It's okay to be attracted to someone with completely different traits than you. Opposites attract!

1. *Personality*

   Are you attracted to someone with a sense of humor? Do you like being around people who are talkers? Do you tend to be a plodder who needs someone who is very spontaneous in your life?

2. *Hobbies*

   Do you want to meet someone who enjoys listening to music or going to the theater? Maybe you want to be with someone who enjoys sightseeing or traveling.

3. *Family*

   If you have children, be sure to meet people who enjoy them. Trust me, both you and your children would be miserable if you were with someone who did not like children.

4. *Physical Traits*

   What are the physical traits that attract you to someone? Do you like someone tall or short? Do you prefer thin or full-figured? Muscular or wiry? Do you find long or short hair sexy?

5. *Travel*

   Are you looking for someone to go boating or cruising with? Do you enjoy international travel, domestic travel, or both? Do you enjoy driving or flying to your destinations?

6. *Religion*

   Is it important to you that your mate be a religious person? Do you want someone with the same spiritual beliefs as you? Do you want your mate to accompany you to religious services?

7. *Sports*

   Do you want someone to play a sport with or who can join you as a spectator? Do you care if your mate watches sports on television? What specific sports do you enjoy?

8. *Health Habits*

   Is it important to you to be with someone who is health-conscious? Do you want someone who has an occasional drink or does it bother you if the person drinks alcohol? Do you care if someone smokes? If it's important then include it on your list.

9. *Exercise*

   Do you exercise regularly and do you want the same in your mate? What form of exercise do you prefer?

10. *Politics*

    Would the fact that someone votes or doesn't vote bother you? Would you be comfortable with a political activist? Does it matter what political party someone prefers?

BE SPECIFIC

When you feel you've included everything you can think of, it's time to narrow your lists down to the basics. Pick a few of your best qualities and then pick the qualities you are seeking in a mate that are most important to you. The more specific you are, the better. Although you may not get as many responses by being very specific as you would with a more general approach, the responses you do get will be a better match for you. Writing a personal ad is a little like advertising an apartment for rent. If you leave out the monthly rent or the address, you'll get too many calls from people who want an apartment in a different price range, or who aren't interested in the area where the apartment is located. By the time the ad expires, you'll be ready to tear your hair out!

The same kind of thing will happen if you leave out your own age or the age-range you're looking for in a mate. You could end up like Rebecca, who was in her early thirties, didn't include her age and got dozens of responses from men in their fifties.

Sally learned her lesson the hard way as well. She spent a lot of time writing a nice, but rather general, ad. In her ad she mentioned that she liked to exercise. She received thirty-five calls in two weeks, but spent much of her time disqualifying many of her calls as she listened to men tell her how they liked to lift weights, ski, and rollerblade. When Sally wrote in her ad that she liked to exercise, she really wanted someone to go country western dancing with her. If she had been specific, she undoubtedly would have had better luck.

Gina, on the other hand, now has a partner to dance with because she advertised for someone who loves swing dancing. She didn't get as many calls as Sally got, but she ended up engaged to one of the men who did respond.

Bill reworded his ad until it was really specific, writing that he was looking for a scuba partner. Not many women responded, but the few who did were exactly what he was looking for.

While I have mentioned several cases of someone looking for a partner to participate in a sport or go dancing, that's certainly not a requirement. Lot's of people are not interested in sports. For example, David was shy and not very athletic. He asked me what to put in his ad, and I told him to just be himself. Here's what he came up with:

STILL WATERS RUN DEEP
Divorced Male, enjoys movies, dinners, and long walks on the beach. Looking for someone who loves children and quiet times.

In two weeks, David got about thirty responses, and he felt good because he didn't have to pretend he was someone else. The women responded to the real David.

Your ad will be effective too, as long as it reflects the real you. For example, Sandy realized that anyone she would be interested in meeting would have to have a good sense of humor. This is what she wrote:

LAUGHING ALL THE WAY
There's laughter in everything. I'm a SWF who enjoys a good ten-mile bike ride. Looking for someone to laugh uphill with.

Sandy was specific about the type of exercise she enjoyed and included humor, a trait that was very important to her. By doing that, she gave her ad a definite personality. You want to catch someone's attention by being yourself. There's no greater feeling than having someone respond to what comes from your heart.

ABBREVIATIONS

As you get into writing your ad, you're going to see that there is one quick way to save money and space, and that's by abbreviating. In the world of personal ads, there is a universal language of abbreviations that you must learn. Usually, the person who takes your ad will be very helpful in this area.

GETTING

CREATIVE

Many people just want the facts and are put off by clever wording. But, there are those people who like something different and are attracted to an ad that shows a little creativity and imagination. All that really matters is that you are comfortable with the ad

COMMONLY USED ABBREVIATIONS	
DWF	Divorced White Female
SWF	Single White Female
DWM	Divorced White Male
SWM	Single White Male
DBF	Divorced Black Female
SBF	Single Black Female
DBM	Divorced Black Male
SBM	Single Black Male
D	Divorced
WW	Widowed Woman
WM	Widowed Man
J	Jewish
A	Asian
NA	Native American
HISP	Hispanic
C	Christian/Catholic
NS	Nonsmoker
S	Smoker
P	Professional
DF	Drug and/or Disease Free

you compose and that it reflects who you really are, as well as the type of person you are looking for. If you're not comfortable with attention-getting phrases, then don't use them. If, on the other hand, you'd like to take a stab at doing something a little different, then let me give you some examples.

BRONCO BUSTER

Can you tame this filly? If you're a tall, attractive, fit SWM, 30–40 years old, and a NS, then this tall, attractive, extremely fit SWF wants to talk to you.

WILMA SEEKS FRED

Attractive, intelligent, classy lady, 49, seeks blue-collar worker to enjoy pleasant entertainment and quiet evenings at home.

BEAM ME UP!

SWF, 43 years old, blonde hair, blue eyes, active mom, a NS. Loves science fiction movies, reading, theater, music, and outdoor activities. Searching universe for male with similar interests. Pointed ears O.K.

SHIPWRECKED

On the mainland P, 5' 3", petite, sexy BF, seeks tall 50+ captain to rescue this first mate back to the islands.

CHECK THIS OUT!

Would you prefer Jack Frost nipping at your nose, or me nuzzling your earlobe. Queen-sized PSBF, 43 years old, searching for x-large PBM, 40–50, who can provide heat this winter.

MR. DISORGANIZED

PDWM, 43, 5' 10", 190#, who thrives on chaos and spontaneity. Kids/humor welcome.

WOLFMAN SEEKS MATE

SBM, 39 years old, likes motorcycles, camping, concerts, trips, quiet times, and of course, haunted houses. So put a spell on me, and let's howl at the moon.

ON THE CRITICAL LIST

Slender, bearded medical SBMP, 50, desires feminine, sexy SBF, 30–50, NS, for relationship of intensive care.

TREASURE HUNT

Attractive, attentive, fun-loving, sincere, SWF seeks SWM, 40+, for friendship first. Are you my pot of gold?

NO CAREER WOMAN!

Same for your independent sisters. Super good-looking SWPM seeks petite, slender, super attractive female, 25–35, to star in a modern version of "Leave It To Beaver."

1945 CADILLAC

Built for comfort not for speed, this well-cared-for black cadillac needs a SBM, 50+, to steer her into a loving relationship down the road of life.

WILL SLAY DRAGONS

This white knight is slender, bearded, medical P, 50. Seeking to win favor of attractive maiden, 35–50, NS, slim to medium build, to be queen of this castle.

Years ago, before there were voice mail messages, people responded to ads by sending letters to a post office box. The following is an example of a woman's positive reaction to a man's creativity. She was so impressed with his creative flair, that she started dating him and they eventually married. This is the ad she submitted:

HETEROSEXUAL FEMALE

Fit, attractive blonde, 5'4" professional, youthful 39, enjoys weekends in the country, weeknights in the city, flowers, music, travel, reading and writing, conversation, the aroma of homemade bread. Is seeking trim, good-looking, personable man with class and depth for friendship and chemistry, sharing and independence. NS, light or non-drinker preferred. Photo.

The man who responded wrote her the following note:

Hi! I think I fit your ad, but came up with this quiz just for fun. My female friends say I should include a picture to show I'm healthy and not scary looking, but I don't have a recent one. I'm looking forward to hearing from you.

He included the following quiz:

Complete the following quiz and return it to me. Check the answer you prefer. If you get a high score, I'm probably your type and you win a phone call or worse, an actual date. If you get a low score, you're also a winner! I'm not your type and you can feel lucky you didn't have a miserable time.

1. *Appearance*
     a. Danny Devito's shorter, uglier brother
     b. 5' 10", 160#, pleasant face, nice hair
     c. 6' 9", 285#, former NFL

2. *Occupation*
     a. 7-11 clerk, graveyard shift
     b. lawyer (don't tell my mother)
     c. trust banker (as in "trust me")
     d. writer

3. *Hobbies*
     a. reading, gardening, theater
     b. watching T.V., drinking good beer
     c. baseball games
     d. playing cards

4. *Financial Status*
     a. not into material things
     b. never filed for bankruptcy
     c. quite comfortable, thanks
     d. Donald Trump's rich uncle

5. *Sports*
     a. golf and dancing
     b. skiing (water and snow), tennis, sailing
     c. turning things over in my mind
     d. skydiving and running

6. *In the Summer I Like to:*
   a. imagine I have a lake cabin
   b. spend long weekends at the lake
   c. visit my lake place which sleeps 38

7. *Marital Status*
   a. divorced (twice)
   b. widower
   c. I'm not sure

8. *When I Travel I Like to Visit:*
   a. campgrounds
   b. my relatives in Iowa
   c. Snowbird, Deer Valley, the Bahamas
   d. some place within walking distance

9. *My Favorite Music Is:*
   a. very eclectic—classical to the Beach Boys
   b. new age
   c. Twisted Sister
   d. "All My Ex's Live In Texas"

10. *At Parties I:*
    a. like to get drunk
    b. enjoy meeting new people
    c. am rather shy
    d. forget where I left my clothes

11. *When I Fall in Love I:*

   a. ask for a free home trial

   b. consider it serious business

   c. want to get married

   d. take the midnight train to Georgia

12. *After Completing this Quiz:*

   a. return it with your photo

   b. return it with someone else's photo

   c. be amazed a grown-up did this

   d. be glad you haven't given your address

The woman responded to the quiz by writing this note:

> Thanks, I enjoyed your creative approach and humor. Here's my photo. See what you think. If you're interested, call me. Evenings are best.

He did, and the rest is history!

BE PREPARED

A person who responds to your ad may request a photo, so you need to be prepared. Before you place your ad, make sure you have a good photo available. If the idea of having your photo taken makes you uncomfortable, I want to urge you to let go of your discomfort and think of it as another part of the adventure. Pretend you are a model and this is a professional photo shoot. Wear something comfortable and flattering, have your hair trimmed or styled, remember to have fun, and feel proud of how you look. You can have a friend take your photo for you or go to a professional photographer. You may even want to go all out and have a glamour photo taken. Just be sure to have copies available when your ad appears.

It's also important to always have a pen and notebook by the phone so you can keep track of each call. You will learn more in the next chapter about record keeping, and believe me, when the calls start coming in, you're going to need some kind of system.

WRITING YOUR AD

By now you have invested a lot of time and thought in considering who you are and what type of person you are looking for. You've also spent a lot of time reading other people's ads. Now it's time to use everything you have learned and write the ad you will place. Whether you decide to use just the facts or get more creative, write your ad as you want it to finally appear.

The next step is to place your ad. You have a choice of publications, including local suburban newspapers and city-wide newspapers. Some cities also have specialty newspapers, or glossy city-magazines. Chances are, your city-wide newspaper will have the most circulation and get the most responses. Depending on your budget, decide which market is best. If you want to and can afford it, you might blitz the area and place your ad in all of the appropriate publications.

The people who take your phone order will help you abbreviate words and condense what you want to say. You'll be given a private access code and a number to call to get your messages. You'll also set up a voice mail message so when someone responds to your ad, they'll hear your voice. (I cover this subject in depth in the next chapter.)

Make sure you record your message as soon as you place your ad. The last thing you want is for interested readers to call and not be able to hear a voice mail message. Being able to have a voice mail message gives you the opportunity to make your first good impression. You can say more about yourself and what you're looking for in a mate than you could in your ad. It gives you another shot at presenting yourself, and at the same time, it further qualifies prospects for a good match. If a person is less attracted to your ad after hearing your voice, then so be it. It only means you're one person closer to meeting your perfect mate!

CHAPTER 3: TAKE ACTION

Below is a summary of the action items described in this chapter. You may want to do all of them now or wait until you have read further. You may want to do some now and some later. There is no right or wrong way. It's entirely up to you. Just remember that if you want to find your dream lover, you have to take action. No more sitting around waiting for the perfect mate to come knocking at your door!

1. Buy publications that carry personal ads. Circle the ads you like and study them.

2. Try writing some practice ads of your own. Don't worry about being too wordy: this is your chance to ask for what you want. You will have time later to revise and perfect your ad. For now, just brainstorm and have fun.

3. Set aside a block of quiet time and using the suggestions in this chapter, complete your personal inventory of traits.

4. Using the same suggestions as a starting point, complete your ideal mate's inventory of traits. Do not feel you need to be limited by my suggestions. If you have additional categories or traits that are important to you, be sure to include them.

5. Using the knowledge you have gained from completing the inventories, write your personal ad, including those traits that are most important to you.

6. Have copies of your photograph available to send to potential dates. If you don't have one you like, get one taken. Don't forget to enjoy the process.

7. Place your ad in the publications you have decided upon.

If you have decided to place a personal ad, congratulations. You have taken an important step in taking control of your life. Have fun and meet as many people as you can.

CHAPTER 4

Voice Mail

DETAILS, DETAILS

Voice mail has changed the entire personal ad industry. Before voice mail, responses to personal ads were mailed to a blind post office box and took days to arrive. With voice mail, you can get a response the same day your ad appears.

When you place your written ad in a publication, you get the opportunity to record a message on your own personal voice mailbox. When someone is interested in your ad, they'll call the publication and be given the "900" number that will let them listen to your voice mail message. This gives them the opportunity to hear your voice and any additional information not supplied in your ad. After listening to your message, they can decide whether or not to leave a message of their own.

While what you say in your written ad is extremely important, your voice mail message is even more crucial. Your voice mail is a wonderful opportunity to elaborate on your ad. You can say much more about yourself and what you're looking for in a mate—and it's in your own voice. This chapter will give you all the information you need to use it to your advantage.

Remember Sid? He was the man who wanted to find a partner with a strong belief in God. He worked hard at being specific in his written ad, but his voice mail message was even more detailed.

Let's look at the difference between Sid's personal ad and his voice mail message. Here's his ad:

> Easy-to-talk-to WM, seeking life partner, age 45–55 with postgraduate degree and strong faith in God.

Now, here's Sid's voice mail message:

> Hello, this is Sid. I mentioned in my ad that I'm easy to talk to. I love to sit over a cup of coffee or tea and share thoughts and feelings about all kinds of topics. I have a master's degree in art history and love to visit art museums and galleries. I have a strong faith in God and want to share my life with someone on the same spiritual path. Please leave a message and indicate the best time to call.

See how your voice mail message can serve to eliminate people who are not a good match? If you were too general in your written ad because of space limitations, you can be much more specific with your voice mail message. It's another opportunity to tell people who you are and what's important to you. And you haven't even talked to them yet!

BE SELECTIVE

What you say in your ad and on your recorded message will go a long way in screening out people who wouldn't be a good match, but you still might get calls from people you aren't interested in dating. If that happens, simply don't return the call. Remember, you're in control. You decide who to interact with.

Carrie put her ad in a local newspaper and felt confident she was specific enough to attract exactly the kind of person she was looking for. Her ad read as follows:

Energetic, Blonde, Petite. Loves biking and hiking. Seeking male age 30–40 to spend time and energy with.

Carrie's voice-mail message restated what she put in her ad, with a little more detail and description to help the caller get to know her better. This is her voice message:

Hi! Thanks for calling. As you can probably tell from my voice, I have a lot of energy. I love to do anything that involves physical activity, especially bike-riding and hiking. I've been climbing and riding all my life, and would love to do that with someone between the ages of 30 and 40. So if you're ready to get some fresh air and good exercise, please leave a message. Thanks again for calling!

She was stunned when her first three callers were in their twenties! Sometimes, even though you've done your best to give as much detail as possible, people ignore what you've said. Perhaps you have stated that you are seeking someone six feet tall or over but you receive messages from men who

are 5'8". Or you state you are looking for blue eyes but someone leaves a message saying theirs are brown. It's up to you to
decide whether you are willing to overlook the differences.
If the person leaving the message has five out of six charac-
teristics you're seeking, you may decide that the one missing
characteristic isn't such a big deal. In that case, call them
back. If, on the other hand, the missing characteristic is very
important, go on to the next message.

That's exactly what Carrie did. She went on to her next
twenty-two messages, and all of them were in the age range
she was looking for.

Think what an effective way this is to save valuable time.
Rather than talking to people who weren't in the age group
she preferred, Carrie took a few minutes to eliminate the
callers she felt were too young for her.

RECORDING YOUR MESSAGE

In today's world of electronics, you've probably already recorded some kind of telephone message. You may have recorded a
greeting on your personal answering machine or a message on
your voice mail at work. Recording a voice mail message for a
personal ad is very similar, except you will include more personal information.

Sid and Carrie worked hard at creating just the right
voice mail message to accompany their ads. Before they
recorded their messages, they wrote down exactly what they
wanted to say. If you want your voice mail message to be
effective, follow their example. If you'll take the time to
think it through and write it down, you can avoid recording

a message filled with long pauses or lots of "ums" and "ahs" as you try to remember what you want to say next. After you've written it down, go back through your script and underline words you want to emphasize or say with a certain inflection or tone. Changing your inflection and emphasizing certain words will give your voice variety and make your message more entertaining.

If you think reading a script will sound phony, just sketch an outline or a list of points you want to make. Using an outline instead of reading your message word-for-word from a script can help you sound more natural. For some of you, looking at key words or phrases may be all you need to get your information across. Whether you use an outline or read your message verbatim, keep your voice upbeat and energetic.

Practice until it sounds natural, aiming for the kind of easy flow that hosts of news shows like *Dateline, 20/20,* or *A Current Affair* achieve as they read the monitor. Their delivery is so natural you can't tell they're reading.

The best advice I can give on recording your voice mail message is to do it with energy, speak clearly, and practice, practice, practice! If you normally speak quite rapidly, practice talking more slowly. A nice conversational pace will work best. Most voice mail services allow a two- to three-minute message, which is plenty of time for what you want to say.

To make the best impression with your message, keep these points in mind:

• Your posture can affect the quality of your voice. Make sure you sit up straight. If you're lying down or slumped over in a chair, your voice will sound tired and weak.

- If you have a cough, a stuffy nose, or don't feel well, wait to record your message. You don't want your callers straining to understand you. It's important to sound your absolute best when recording your voice.

- Smile while you're recording your message. You will automatically sound more energetic and cheerful.

Telemarketers know how important it is to smile while they talk to a customer. Part of their training often includes placing a mirror on the desk in front of them and smiling into the mirror as they speak. When you smile, you sound friendly and people will respond to you in a friendly way.

Practice saying the following sentence, first without a smile, then with one. "Hi, I'm (your name) and I'm so glad you called!"

Can you hear the difference? Use this technique for every message you record and I'll bet people will comment on how cheerful you sound.

MAKE IT PERSONAL

Your ad and your voice mail message are meant to complement each other. While your written ad consists of hard data and objective information, your voice mail shows your personal side. Marlene's ad and voice mail message are a good example of how your voice mail can give added insight into your personality. In her ad, she wrote:

Striking Brunette, age 39, loves people. Seeks potential mate who likes children and animals.

As a followup, Marlene recorded this voice mail message:

> Thanks for calling "Striking Brunette." I'm happy you
> called. Being brunette isn't the only thing that makes
> me striking. I have a warm, engaging personality, and I
> care a lot about people. I love all living creatures, but
> my favorites are children and animals. I volunteer a lot
> of my time at Children's Hospital and at the zoo. I'm
> looking for a man with an open heart and lots of com-
> passion to share my love of giving.

Can you see how Marlene's voice mail message expanded on
her ad and made her more real? While her ad mentioned that
she loved people, her recorded message showed she was sincere. Her devotion to volunteer work demonstrated she was a
caring and compassionate woman.

Like Marlene, compose your ad to show the outer you
and let your recorded message portray the inner you. This
combination will give a well-rounded picture of who you
are, what's important to you, and what you're looking for
in a mate.

Another reason to share more of yourself in your voice
mail message is to encourage your caller to do the same.
If your message is brief and unrevealing, chances are the
responses you receive will be the same. While you want your
callers to leave basic information such as age, physical description, hobbies and so on, you can encourage them to reveal
more of themselves by setting an example.

Try to avoid making the same mistake as Ralph—a man of
few words. His ad and his voice mail were very brief and so
were the responses. Ralph didn't understand that if he wanted

to learn something about his callers, he had to let them learn about him. His ad read like this:

> Nice Guy. Blonde male, age 48, seeking woman to spend quality time with.

His voice mail simply reiterated what was in his written ad:

> It's true. I'm a nice guy and I'd like to get to know you. So please leave a message.

His short message actually discouraged people from leaving messages and the few calls he did receive mirrored the same kind of message he gave. The whole idea of using voice mail is to qualify yourself to others and narrow your prospects, an impossible task with such scant information. If you use your recorded message to zero in on the things that are important, you'll save time and money, returning only the calls with the most potential.

GETTING ORGANIZED

Being prepared is essential to running a successful personal ad campaign. The more organized you are, the more successful you'll be. If you were searching for a job, your strategy would include some kind of record-keeping system. You'd keep track of your interviews, how many résumés you sent out, key contacts at each company, and how many times you called. Without a system, your job search would be completely disorganized and it would be difficult, if not impossible, to remain on track.

Finding your lifetime partner is the most important search you'll ever make, so you must be even more organized than when searching for a job. The following tips will help you organize your search and maximize your results:

- Get a notebook or journal to use exclusively for logging notes and records on personal ads. Don't use a book that you use for something else. It won't be long before your book is completely filled with names and information. Whatever you do, avoid writing your notes on scraps of paper, thinking you'll transfer them to your notebook later. If you're like most people, you'll lose the scrap of paper or forget to record it in your logbook.

- Keep a copy of each ad, where it was placed, and when it expires. Remember, when your ad expires, your voice mail also expires and your personal ad campaign comes to a screeching halt!

- Be sure to overlap your ads so when one expires, you have another one in place. This way, you'll never lose momentum in your search.

- Keep a record of your access codes. When you run an ad, the publication provides an access code for your voice mailbox. If you're running ads in different publications, each ad will have a different access code. If you forget your code, you can't get your messages.

- When you get your access code, record your message immediately to activate your voice mail. The last thing you want is for people to call and not get a message.

- Take notes on every call, even if it's from someone you don't expect to call back. As you listen, write down the information. Instead of writing every word, record important phrases or words. For example, your notes might look something like this: Jim, 241-8906. Likes sailing, never married. Age 34.

- Always leave a few spaces after your notes from each call. That way, if you return the call, you'll have room for notes during your conversation.

- You'll need a system to rate the messages you receive. You could use a scale of one to five, highlighting messages with different colored markers or placing stickers next to the best of them. It doesn't matter what you do, but you do need a way to remind yourself which callers have top priority.

Judith didn't think about rating her calls when she came home from work the day after placing her ad and dialed her access code. Thrilled to find over thirty messages, she quickly wrote down a little bit of information as she listened to each message. When she had finished listening to all her messages, she had some information on each of them but had forgotten which calls were her favorites. Fortunately, she hadn't erased any of the messages, so she was able to listen to them again, this time putting a plus sign next to the most interesting ones. But it took twice as long as it should have by the time she finished listening to them.

SAVE YOUR LOGBOOK

Whatever you do, keep your notebook or journal. You never know when you might need to refer to it again.

Gene met Naomi through the personals and dated her for six months. After that time, Naomi was transferred out of the area and their relationship ended. When Naomi left, Gene went back to his notebook instead of placing another ad. He had been careful to prioritize his calls and there were several marked as interesting prospects. Gene began calling the names marked with a star. The first two women he called were already dating someone, but the third woman had just ended a relationship and was happy to talk with him. They set up a time to meet and have been dating ever since.

Another reason to keep your notebook is that you might get a call from someone you wouldn't want to date, but who might be perfect for one of your friends.

Jillian ran a personal ad that specifically said she didn't want to get involved with someone with children. One of the forty-plus calls she received was from Marvin, a man with a six-year-old son. He thought because he had only one child, Jillian might reconsider. She didn't reconsider, but after she hung up, she thought of a friend she knew who would be happy to date someone with children. Jillian called her friend and shared the information she had noted from the call. Her friend was interested, so Jillian called Marvin and suggested that he might want to call her friend. He did and he and Jillian's friend are now married.

Another reason to save your notebook is to determine whether or not someone has called before. If you don't return all of your calls—and you're not obligated to do so—you might get more than one call from the same person. If you get a call from someone who sounds familiar, you'll be able to review your records to see if the person called you before.

TRUST YOUR INTUITION

To screen and rate your calls, you'll have to listen very carefully to each message. I don't mean just listening to the caller's words, but listening to what's said between the lines. To do this, you have to listen with your heart as well as your head.

The first step to good listening is giving your full attention to what's being said. Pick a time to listen when you won't be distracted, rushed, or interrupted and be sure you're not too tired to concentrate. Replay each message as many times as it takes to get it all down. Sometimes it's hard to catch everything the first time you listen to a message. The caller may speak too fast or leave so much detail that you miss something the first time through. Be careful not to erase the message until you've gotten everything you need from it.

When you're in a position to concentrate, focus, and listen, you'll be able to tell a lot by a caller's tone of voice, inflection, and energy level. Listen for all of these things and follow your intuition. If there's something about the person's voice that bothers you, then listen to your gut feeling and don't call back. If, on the other hand, the caller gives you minimal information but your instincts tell you to go ahead, return the call.

Pay attention to your first impression of a caller—it's often very accurate. If you start talking yourself into calling someone back that initially turned you off, pay attention. Remember, a personal ad gives you lots of options. There are plenty of calls to choose from, so don't respond to a call if it doesn't feel right.

Rosemary had more than fifteen messages in her voice mailbox the day after she ran her personal ad. After listening to her third message, she replayed it a few more times. The man's message included everything she was looking for. He was in his thirties, had a corporate job, and loved boating, but there was something in his voice that made her uncomfortable. When he ended his message with, "So, sweetheart, when you get a chance, call me," she cringed. Rosemary spent twenty minutes trying to convince herself to call this man, but couldn't get over her negative feelings about his tone of voice and the "sweetheart." It finally dawned on Rosemary that she was spending too much time on this one message, when she had sixteen other calls from prospects, and she went on to the next call.

Like Rosemary, you will have times when your instincts tell you not to respond to a particular call. When this happens, trust your intuition. There will also be times when you just can't decide whether to respond to a call or not. Perhaps, for every quality you like in the caller, there's a quality you're not sure about. If you find yourself straddling the fence on a particular caller, I suggest that you go ahead and phone. It may take a little extra time, but by calling you'll know for sure whether the caller is a prospect or not. If you don't interview the person, you'll always wonder what would have happened if you had called.

Another tip to help you screen callers is to return their call when you think they won't be home. By listening to a person's voice on a personal answering machine, you can learn more than you might have learned from the message the caller left on your voice mail.

For example, Harvey received a message from a woman who sounded a little nervous and unsure of herself. Although she stammered a lot during her message, something in her voice sounded so sincere that Harvey decided to call her answering machine during the day. When he did, he heard the same woman, but she sounded completely different. Her voice was perky, energetic, and filled with confidence and Harvey was glad he had called her when she wasn't home so he could hear her true voice.

Once you've listened to all your messages and have ranked them according to your interest level, you're ready to start returning calls. Call the people you're most interested in promptly. If you wait too long to call, they may hook up with someone else before you reach them.

After you've finished your top-priority calls, make your "middle of the road" calls. These are the people you'll have to interview to know for sure whether or not you'll want to meet them. It's in this category that you'll eliminate a lot of prospects. The ones you eliminate will go into the "never in a million years" category. That doesn't mean there's anything wrong with these callers, they're just not the right match for you.

PHONE INTERVIEWS

When you have listened to all of your messages and decided on which calls to return, you're ready to conduct a phone interview. A phone interview is your last chance to learn more about someone before you decide whether to meet the person. Although the interview process takes time, it's well worth it. If you don't conduct a thorough enough interview, you may discover later you've wasted time dating someone who isn't a good match for you.

Randy learned this lesson the hard way. He had gotten some information about Carla on the voice mail message she left him. Even though he intended to learn more about her in a phone interview, he ended up making a date with her just two minutes into their conversation and then hanging up. He was so taken by Carla's alluring voice that he couldn't imagine she'd be someone he wouldn't want to meet.

When they met, Randy quickly realized he hadn't devoted enough time to his phone interview with her. Carla's voice was still alluring, but the fact that she had three very young children wasn't. Randy liked children, but he wasn't ready to get involved with someone with that many little ones. If Randy had taken the time to conduct a more thorough interview, he wouldn't have wasted an evening out with someone who wasn't a good match for him.

Before you make the call to interview someone, you need to invest some time preparing. Remember the questionnaires you completed earlier about yourself and what you're looking for in a mate? Study this information now, and use it as an aid to compose the questions you'll ask in the interview. How your prospects answer these questions will help you decide whether or not they're good candidates for a mate.

In the personal ad game, the rules are different than they would be in a social encounter. It's assumed that both parties want to learn as much about each other as possible before they decide to meet face-to-face. So questions like, "Do you attend church regularly?" "Do you think you'll ever want to have children?" or "Do you own your own home?" are perfectly acceptable. Your phone interview is not the time for small talk. There's an unspoken rule that phone interviews are the time for gathering information and qualifying, so don't hold back. Ask whatever questions you feel are necessary to get the information that will help you find your mate.

It's understandable that you might feel a little nervous when you talk to someone for the first time. If so, it might help to remember that he or she called *you*. They saw something in your ad and heard something in your voice that they liked, so take a deep breath and enter this next stage with a feeling of confidence. If you let your nervousness get the best of you, it will interfere with your ability to concentrate on the important questions you need to ask and to focus on the answers. If you're worried about the impression you're making, you won't be able to follow your intuition. Besides, the person you're interviewing is probably as nervous as you are. So, if their voice cracks or they stutter, be patient.

Just as you picked a quiet time to listen to your voice mail messages, you need to set aside time when you won't be interrupted, when you're ready to conduct your phone interview. If your dog is barking or your roommate is running the disposal, it will be impossible to pay attention to the answers to your questions.

IT'S NOT WHAT YOU SAY, IT'S HOW YOU SAY IT

It's very important to start your interview in a positive way. I suggest you begin by thanking the person for taking interest in your ad and asking a few warm-up questions about his or her experience with personal ads to break the ice. Then move on to your specific questions, remembering that the other person wants to know about you as much as you want to know about him or her.

When questioning someone, it's okay to be direct, but be careful not to come across as if you are interrogating the person. This is supposed to be a friendly exchange of information, not a police investigation. As with any kind of communication, it's not what you say, but how you say it, that counts. When asking a question, ask it without being judgmental. You can get the facts without telling a person they're right or wrong.

When Celeste called Herb for a phone interview, she asked him about his career. When he told her he was an attorney, she said, "Oh, I see" in a disappointed voice, since she was interested in meeting someone in the corporate world. The rest of the conversation was very uncomfortable for both of them.

If, during the interview, you learn something about the other person that you don't like, simply make a note of it in your logbook, but keep your disapproval to yourself. If what you hear is unacceptable, you can quickly but politely end the conversation. Try to end all of your conversations on a positive note by thanking the person for his or her time.

Although it's important to listen to your intuition when a caller sounds completely wrong for you, I want to caution you against over-screening callers to the point that you end up eliminating everyone. Stay firm on finding someone who shares your values and goals, but try to be flexible in areas of less importance, such as hobbies and interests. For instance, if you went fishing once and didn't enjoy it, and you interview someone who likes to fish, don't throw away the chance to meet the person just because of one negative experience. You never know, the next time you go fishing you might catch your lifelong mate!

Once you start talking with the other person, it's likely the conversation will either flow easily or it will feel like you're pulling teeth. If it's awkward and uncomfortable, or if you find you have nothing in common, it's probably useless to set up a meeting. If, on the other hand, conversation flows, there's a comfortable give and take and some humor, you'll want to arrange to meet.

Remember, always pick a place to meet that's public and busy, and always provide your own transportation. Do not give out your phone number and address until you are positive you want to see this person again.

PRACTICE MAKES PERFECT

By the way, don't worry about blowing it. You've never done this before. The more you do it, the easier it will become. Just like a job interview, the first time is pretty scary, but by the twentieth interview, you know exactly what to say. What's important is to have fun and meet as many people as you can. And be sure to send me an invitation to your wedding, when you meet and marry the mate of your dreams!

CHAPTER 4: TAKE ACTION

Now that you have finished reading this chapter, you are ready to place your ad and record your voice mail message. Remember, this is a grand adventure. Be prepared to respond to many messages from more people interested and eager to meet you than you ever dreamed possible.

1. Using the guidelines in this chapter, write your voice mail message. Be sure to use your message to enlarge on the information in your ad and to personalize it.

2. Practice smiling as you say your message out loud until it sounds smooth and natural.

3. When you are satisfied with your delivery, record your message. Don't forget to smile.

4. Get a log or notebook to be used exclusively for tracking and recording responses.

5. Listen to your messages when you won't be distracted and rate each call according to your level of interest.

6. Prepare questions for your phone interviews using the personal inventories completed in chapter 3.

7. Respond right away to the callers who interest you the most. Then proceed to call the rest of the people you wish to interview.

8. If a caller is someone you think may be a good match for you, set up a meeting. Be sure to schedule it in a busy, public place and get there using your own transportation. Do not reveal the phone number or address

at either your home or workplace until you are certain this is someone you wish to see again.

Your voice mail message is your chance to let your caller know a more personal you. Use your positive self-image to present yourself with warmth and confidence.

Dating Services

ON-LINE DATING

In recent years, on-line dating services have made their debut. Computers have become almost as common as the telephone, and people are looking to the information super-highway to find their perfect mate. If you have a computer, all you'll need is a modem and an Internet service provider to join the exciting world of on-line dating. There are many companies that can hook you up to the Internet, all charging roughly the same price. If you don't have a computer yet, this might be the perfect time to purchase one since prices keep coming down, making them very affordable. If owning a computer is out of the question for you, it is still possible to use the Internet by visiting the library, the larger copy centers, or one of the new coffeehouses that provide computers and Internet access for an hourly fee.

In general, on-line dating services are considerably less expensive than other types of dating services and are certainly the most convenient. Getting a description of the membership options, submitting your information, picking your potential dates and payment can all be done right on your computer from your home or office. They use what is called a "secure server" so your information remains confidential. Filling out a questionnaire on-line is similar to doing it in the office of a dating service. They want to know your interests and values and what it is you want in a mate.

Another big benefit of using an on-line dating service is that your membership is worldwide. With the international access of the Internet, you are able to meet people from almost any country. Granted, not everyone wants to start a relationship with someone thousands of miles away, but for some an international or long-distance relationship is very appealing.

Eric, for example, loved to travel and experience different cultures. He found the idea of meeting someone from a foreign country and going to visit them very exciting, so he became a member of an on-line dating service. As a member, he was able to read on-line profiles of women from other countries. When he found someone interesting, he would e-mail her to see if they were compatible. That's how Eric connected with Sonia, who lived in Moscow. He and Sonia spent weeks learning about each other on-line. They shared their travel histories, family backgrounds, religious beliefs, and even their photos. After three months talking on the Internet, they agreed to meet in London.

Sonia and Alex toured London together for three days and spent the next few days in Paris. Before parting, Sonia asked Eric to make his next trip a visit to her in Russia. He met her there two months later, they got married, and Eric remains in Moscow with Sonia.

If you know you don't want a long-distance relationship, be sure you specify in your ad exactly where you're located. Make it very clear that you only want to date someone who is in your vicinity.

Donna lived in Evanston, Illinois, and was interested in meeting someone who lived within a two-hundred-mile radius of her home. However, when she signed up with an on-line dating service, she neglected to mention that. Although she had over seventy responses to her ad, only three were from Illinois.

Many on-line dating services offer "chat rooms" where members can talk to other members. A chat room provides a wonderful forum for people to get to know each other and decide whether or not they want to continue their relationship. Part of the beauty of meeting through a chat room is that it takes the relationship out of the realm of the physical and into something more intimate. You come to know what a person is really like without being influenced by his or her physical appearance. When you meet, there may be some adjustments to make in order to reconcile your expectations with reality; but since you are already friends, you will be far more tolerant.

Vivian met Carlton in a chat room. They both were comfortable using the chat room because they felt they could take as much time as they wanted to get to know one another. After a few conversations, they agreed to exchange photos of themselves, and although neither looked as the other expected, they continued their on-line relationship and eventually decided to meet. Carlton lived in New York and Vivian's home was in Ohio, so they decided to meet at a point in Pennsylvania, halfway between their homes. For Carlton and Vivian, getting acquainted in a chat room made their first face-to-face meeting an event they could look forward to with confidence.

MEETING THROUGH THE INTERNET

The Internet is especially appealing for people who are normally shy in person-to-person situations. On the Internet, you have the opportunity to think about what you want to say, type it, and then edit it if it doesn't come out the way you want. Many people find it more comfortable to express themselves through writing than through speaking. Men, in particular, seem to like the anonymity of the Internet. Talking to someone on the Net is much like writing in a diary or talking to yourself. People tend to reveal more of themselves and their feelings because they feel safe. No one knows your identity.

By the same token, some people may be more likely to lie about themselves, so it's important to check a person out thoroughly before you agree to meet him or her. Here are some important points to remember when meeting someone on the Internet:

- Be honest about yourself. Remember, you are perfect just as you are. If you aren't honest, how do you expect to find the perfect person for you?

- Don't reveal too much about yourself until you know the person well and know that he or she is trustworthy. (In the movie *You've Got Mail* Meg Ryan and Tom Hanks used ficticious names instead of their real names and always stuck to their rule of *no specifics.*) You might feel more comfortable if you ask for a picture, and you will certainly want to talk on the phone before meeting.

• Beware of life stories that seem too sensational, fascinating, or exciting. If it sounds too good to be true, it probably is. This is good advice, regardless of how you meet.

• Use the same common-sense approach to an actual meeting as you would toward someone you met through the personal ads. Meet during the day, in a public place, and take a friend if it feels more comfortable to you.

Another option for personals on the Internet is to create your own home page on the World Wide Web. There are software packages to enable you to create your own Web page or you can hire a professional Web site designer. You can make your Web page as simple or elaborate as you like. You can scan your photo onto the page and even include graphics and background music. Depending on your budget, you can get as creative as you want.

Walter, who was creative and good with computers, had a lot of fun designing his own personal Web page. He did everything he could think of to lure people to his "web." He had a graphic artist design a picture of his head attached to a spider's body. Graphics of spider webs and different kinds of spiders were strategically placed throughout his Web site and his background music was "The Itsy Bitsy Spider." Because of his creativity, he attracted close to a hundred Web surfers a week.

Many revisited his site just to see what crazy thing he'd have on his page next.

Walter lured one visitor into his web that he never let go. Of course, she didn't put up much of a fight. Walter and Veronica were married a year after they met on the Internet.

I have developed an on-line dating service that you can access through my Web site at: www.lightyourfire.com. The *Light Your Fire* dating service is a private, on-line dating club where people meet, connect, and just plain have fun. We offer a free trial to invite you to experience some of the club's main features. We do offer a full membership that includes services beyond that of the free trial. There is a small fee for these additional services. All the information you provide is kept strictly confidential. When you use e-mail within the system, other users will never know who you are, or know your real e-mail address, unless you tell them.

Although we offer an excellent on-line dating service, there are many other dating services available on the Internet. To find additional services, just type in "dating services" in an Internet search and you will find numerous listings.

There are services that specialize in certain subjects or areas of interest. Other services focus on specific religions, education, age groups, and so on. Browse through the various other dating services and remember you can always be a member of more than one service and maximize your on-line dating experience. I recommend that you find a service that offers a free trial period so that you can explore whether it is the type of service you are looking for.

TRADITIONAL DATING SERVICES

Using a traditional dating service is more expensive than placing a personal ad or using the Internet, but it's an excellent alternative if you can afford it.

There are many good reasons to use a traditional dating service. Lots of people use them because they're just too busy to search for a mate themselves. If your lifestyle is such that you don't have time to write an ad, record a voice mail message, or follow up on messages, then a dating service may be just what you're looking for. Although you will have to devote some time initially to complete a questionnaire and be interviewed, if you join a service with experienced matchmakers, you should have to do very little else.

Marianne was a partner in a law firm, as well as president of a professional organization. Between court cases and committee meetings, she barely had time to eat and sleep. Too busy to organize a game plan for meeting new people herself, Marianne joined a dating service. The hour or so Marianne had to devote to being interviewed and filling out a questionnaire was well worth it compared to the time she saved by having the dating service match her up with compatible people.

People who are new to an area and don't know many people are also inclined to use a dating service. Tom transferred from a small town to a large city and knew absolutely no one when he moved into his apartment. He was an accountant for a small family business and spent most of his time either at the office or in his apartment. He signed up with a dating service, met someone he liked, and within a month, had a wonderful circle of friends.

CHOOSING THE RIGHT TYPE
OF SERVICE

There are several types of dating services. Which kind you use depends on how much you want to be involved in the match-making process and how much money you want to spend.

One kind is a computerized dating service. You're asked to fill out a questionnaire describing yourself and the kind of person you want to meet. The information is then entered into a computer, which searches its data bank for compatible profiles. The computer doesn't interpret your data. It simply takes your information and matches it to someone else's.

Colleen, a shy woman who was extremely uncomfortable meeting new people, hadn't been on a date in almost a year. She became so worried about it that she started seeing a counselor. After a couple of sessions, the counselor suggested Colleen sign up with a dating service. At first, Colleen was horrified. She felt that dating services were for losers, but when her counselor told her about another client who had used a dating service and was now happily married, Colleen changed her mind. She finally concluded that she didn't have anything to lose, so she called the dating service and made an appointment.

Colleen signed up for a fifteen-month membership which allowed her to receive two matching profiles a month. First she had to fill out a questionnaire, answer some essay questions about her interests and values, and get her photo taken. Her profile was matched and mailed to two other members each month, and Colleen received two profiles each month from men who were found to be compatible. When she received a matching profile, she decided whether or not to call the person. If she called, and the call went well, she would make a date to meet for coffee as suggested by the service.

After dates with five different men she met through the service, Colleen received a call from Andy whose file she had just received that day. After two phone calls, they agreed to meet for dinner. They had a wonderful time at dinner and continued seeing each other. On their sixth date, Andy shyly asked Colleen if she wanted to go "inactive." Colleen's heart skipped a beat as she quickly answered, "Yes!" In the dating service world, "going inactive" is the same as going steady. It means you want to take your name off the service's active file. In other words, you've found someone wonderful!

Colleen and Andy never went back on the active list. They are now happily married and have two children, a dog, and a turtle.

A second type of dating service provides a more personal touch. This type is called "hand matching." Instead of feeding your information from your questionnaire directly into a computer, it is taken during a personal interview. The person conducting the interview asks you to list your attributes and what attributes you are looking for in a mate. The matching process is based not only on the information you give but also on the interviewer's intuition. This kind of dating service claims they do a better job than a computerized service because they are more subjective and personal. You'll pay more for this kind of service than for a computerized one.

Morgan joined this type of dating service but didn't ask if the person interviewing him would be the one matching him up with appropriate dates. The interviewer spent an hour with Morgan learning all about his interests, values, and goals, and what he was looking for in a mate. Morgan left the dating service feeling that they knew exactly what kind of person he was looking for. What Morgan didn't know was that the interviewer handed his paperwork over to someone else to do the matching.

The person who received Morgan's paperwork was very busy that day. She saw the name Morgan and assumed it was a woman's name. As unbelievable as it sounds, Morgan's profile was matched to a man's instead of a woman's. You can imagine his reaction when he got a phone call from another man explaining that he was matched up to him. Luckily, he had a good sense of humor and was able to straighten it out with the dating service.

Jean's experience with a similar kind of service was much smoother. The dating service she joined "hand-matched" her to a man who eventually became her husband. What she liked most about the dating service was the personal attention she received. She and her interviewer built a good rapport right away. Jean felt her interviewer understood exactly the kind of person she was looking for, and she confirmed that her interviewer would be the person doing the matching.

During the three months she used the dating service, Jean met several men and had a lot of fun. The fourth man she met is now her husband. Jean says she almost didn't join the dating service, thinking it was too expensive; now every time she looks at her husband and two children, she's very glad she did.

To benefit most from this kind of service, it's important that the person who interviews you is the same one who matches you. If your paperwork goes to someone who's never met you but who tries to match you up, your chances for a

good match diminish. The person who's only seen your paperwork doesn't know you as well, so always ask the interviewer
if he or she will be doing the matching. If not, insist on a personal meeting with the person who will.

The next kind of dating service is classified as "self-service."
In this kind of dating service, there are two categories: profile
dating and video dating. These services are among the most
time-consuming of all the services. Each time you want to
look at a person's profile or video, you have to take the time
to travel to the dating service offices, but many people feel the
time is well spent.

As a member of a profile dating service, you get the opportunity to look at a group of files and choose which people you
want to contact. At the same time, other members have the
chance to look at your file and decide whether they want to
call you. While it is more time-consuming than the process
involved in some of the other types of dating services, this
process puts you in control of the search process.

Some people, like Katie, don't want to rely on anyone else's
interpretation of the data. Katie liked using a profile dating
service because she felt a greater sense of control. She liked to
review each profile herself to see which ones she felt best
defined her ideal mate. It was while studying profiles that she
came upon Noel's, which happened to include a photo. Katie
liked what she saw and she also liked the fact that Noel was a
member of the Sierra Club. Katie loved hiking and climbing,
and until then she hadn't found anyone who enjoyed those
activities as much she did. Noel sounded like a very good
prospect. For Katie, the best thing about the profile dating service was the feeling of having a hand in creating her own destiny.

The second type of self-service dating service is video dating. Watching a video gives you a much better sense of people than is possible from reading their file or looking at their picture.

By watching a video, you get to see how people present themselves. Body language, posture, facial expressions, and gestures can tell a lot about a person. How a person says something can be more revealing than what they say. Tone of voice and inflection give clues to a person's true feelings. When viewing a video, keep in mind that the person may appear a little nervous, which is only natural under the circumstances. In general, though, you'll get a good feel for someone's personality by watching his or her video.

Eleanor joined a video dating service even though she knew it was more expensive than the profile dating service. It was worth the extra cost to her to be able to hear and see a man before she met him. When Eleanor viewed Sam's video, she liked what she saw, even though he looked a little older than the age she preferred. Eleanor says his sincerity and sense of humor made her smile the whole time she watched his five-minute video. She told the service to let him know she wanted to meet him.

The service called Sam to tell him about Eleanor and invite him to their office to view Eleanor's tape. He went in right away and loved what he saw. Sam called her that night and they set up a time to meet.

On their first date, their shared experience of making a video made Sam and Eleanor feel they had something in common right away. Each time they went on another date they discovered more that they shared. They had both grown up on Long Island, they both were only children, and they had both undergone knee surgery. After just twelve dates, Sam and Eleanor were looking through travel magazines to decide where to go on their honeymoon.

Another type of dating service is a professional search agency. These agencies are like head hunters for your love life. They're much more expensive than computer, profile, or video services, but you get very individualized treatment, including your own consultant who places ads and does all the networking for you.

Melinda was the chief financial officer for a large corporation and didn't have the time to even think about placing an ad, much less qualify the people who responded to it. For her, a professional search agency was perfect. She had one interview with a consultant and was told that as soon as they had a match they would call her.

Two weeks later, the agency called her with the profile of a man named Mike, who they felt would be a great match for her. She read through Mike's file and called him. They hit it off on the phone and made a date to go to the ballet the following week.

DO YOUR HOMEWORK

When looking for a dating service, it's important to shop around. Investigate as many agencies as possible to find the one that best fits your particular needs. For instance, if seeing the person is important to you, you probably want a video service or one that supplies photos. If you have limited time or have to drive long distances, a computer service might be best for you.

Remember, this is an investment in your future. You need to know exactly what you're getting for your money. Do your homework before you get caught up in a sales pitch. When you call for information, be prepared to ask lots of questions and always ask for a brochure. The following are some questions you should always ask a dating service:

- *What types of memberships are offered?*
  Sometimes they offer both short-term and long-term memberships. When Alex was looking for a dating service, he wanted a short-term membership because he knew he was going to be transferred out of the area in six months.

- *How many years have they been in business?*
  Feel free to check their record with the Better Business Bureau.

- *How many active members do they have?*
  They may have a membership of 3,000 people, but only have 100 active members.

- *If you meet someone you like, can you put your membership on hold or get a pro-rated refund?*

- *What percent of active members are in the age range you prefer?*
  Even though the service might have 1,200 active members, only 2 percent of them might be in your age range.

- *Ask for references from past customers.*
  The dating service should be happy to give you names of satisfied customers.

No matter what type of dating service you decide to use, it's always important to get a written contract signed by both yourself and the agency. Be as specific as possible in the contract. For example, have the specific criteria you're unwilling to compromise on in the contract, as well as the minimum number of introductions you'd like during your membership. When deciding on how long a contract to sign, be realistic. A dating service can't work miracles in a short amount of time. I always suggest people sign a contract of at least one year.

BE PREPARED

Once you've chosen a dating service, be prepared to complete a questionnaire and be interviewed. You'll be asked to answer questions about your age, weight, interests, values, health background, financial status, and so on. Some of these questions may seem rather personal, but remember, the service needs the information to be able to make the best match for you. To help you to be as thorough as possible, take along the evaluations you completed earlier about yourself and what you're looking for in a mate.

Before joining any dating service, make a list of criteria on which you're unwilling to compromise. For example, if you absolutely won't date someone who smokes, put that down. If you'll only date someone who enjoys children, be sure to include it. Obviously, you can't ask the agency to meet every single one of your criteria, but there may be a handful of qualities you want in someone that are so important you won't bend. Know what those qualities are before you talk to a dating service and be sure they provide a written statement saying they will meet those specific criteria.

For example, when he met with the representative from a computer dating service, Neal explained that he would not, under any circumstances, date someone who smoked or wasn't Jewish. However, he made the mistake of not getting a written agreement from the dating service stating that they would meet his two criteria. Within the first month, Neal was given several matches, but the ones who were Jewish smoked, and the ones who didn't smoke weren't Jewish. He wasted a lot of time going in circles with the customer service person because he had not gotten a written agreement.

Some dating services give a personality profile test. These tests are used to match you up with someone compatible. If you take one of these, you're entitled to see your score and the scores of anyone you'll be introduced to, so don't be afraid to ask to examine them.

DOCUMENT YOUR DATES

Whenever you meet someone the service has matched you with, make sure to keep records of your meetings. If you're unhappy with a particular match, you'll want to be able to tell the service why. If you're seeing one or two people a week, and you don't keep a record of each meeting, it'll be hard for you to remember which person had what qualities.

Connie documented all of her face-to-face meetings and was glad she did when she had to explain to the dating service how terribly mismatched she was on one occasion. Connie was very petite and had specifically asked for a man who was no taller than 5' 8". He also needed to be a nonsmoker and someone who enjoyed dancing. Somehow the dating service matched her up with a man who was 6' 2", smoked, and whose favorite pastime was playing computer games. As soon as she got home from her date with him, she wrote down every detail she could remember. The next day, she called her interviewer and told her about the mismatch. Her interviewer apologized profusely and gave her two extra introductions at no charge.

Be aware ahead of time that mix-ups will occur. Depending on how large the dating service is, they may be dealing with thousands of members. Before signing a contract, ask what kind of compensation they provide for mismatches. If you know what they'll do to rectify their mistakes ahead of time, you'll avoid hearing, "We're sorry, but there's nothing we can do."

If you choose an agency that requires an interview, I want you to take it as seriously as you would a job interview. The match you get will depend a lot on the kind of impression you make, so put your best foot forward and remember to confirm that the person who interviews you is the one who does the matching.

MAKE YOURSELF MEMORABLE

Interviewers see people all day long, one right after the other, so it helps to make yourself memorable in some way. For example, Samantha wore a sweater that she had designed and made herself on the day of her interview. The instant Samantha walked in, her interviewer complimented her on her unique sweater. When she learned that Samantha had made it herself, the interviewer was so impressed she asked if Samantha would make her a similar one. Samantha had cleverly succeeded in making a lasting and favorable impression.

Another thing to look for in a dating service is whether or not they have a newsletter. Many dating services publish a newsletter as a communications tool, using it to update members on changes in the company and to notify them of upcoming events. This can be a very useful way to stay informed without having to spend time making calls to the service for information.

USE THE COUNSELORS

Some services also have counselors as part of their customer service department. Depending on the size of the dating service, there should be one or more people with matchmaking experience available to answer your questions whenever they come up.

Gretchen had never used a dating service before, and was thrilled when she was matched for the first time. She went on a few dates with the man the service matched her up with and got along very well with him. Because he was a good match and she felt they really had a chance at a future together, she began thinking she should go ahead and cancel her membership. Not sure what she should do, Gretchen remembered being told that the service had several relationship advisors if she ever needed one. She called customer service and explained her dilemma to one of the counselors. Although the counselor was happy that Gretchen was satisfied with her match, she advised her that it was too soon to end her search. On the advice of the counselor, Gretchen decided to keep her membership active and was glad she did when the man she had been dating got a job transfer and had to move away just a couple of weeks later.

As a recap, here are the most important things to look for in any dating service:

- A written contract, including as many specifics as possible

- Current clients who are happy with the service

- A customer service department with experienced relationship counselors

- An interview with the person who will do your matchmaking

If the service you choose meets at least these four conditions, you can feel pretty certain you'll have a positive experience. Remember, the more questions you ask and the more research you do, the more satisfied you'll feel, even if you don't find a perfect match right away.

Gary signed up for a fifteen-month membership with a video dating service, but not before he asked every question he could possibly think of. Before signing on the dotted line, he made sure the company had a customer service department to help him in selecting the most appropriate videos to view. He asked how many active members there were in his age group. He inquired about whether the service provided social functions and if they were included in his membership or were at an extra cost. He asked if he could put his membership on hold or get a refund if he met someone before his membership expired. He even asked if the service had a payment program. He left no stone unturned so that when he finally did decide to join the service, he felt as informed as he possibly could. Even after having done all of his research, it still took nine months for Gary to meet the woman he eventually married. Looking back on it, he said that if he hadn't been as well informed, he probably would have become frustrated and dropped out of the service after a few months— and missed meeting the love of his life!

YOUR MONEY OR YOUR TIME

Whether you decide to run your own customized dating service by designing a personal Web page, join an independent dating service, or hire a personal search agency, you'll create opportunities to meet the people that are right for you. Yes, using a dating service does require a financial commitment, but you must accept the fact that when looking for a mate, you'll have to spend either your time or your money. As you will learn in later chapters, there are many, many ways to meet people that don't cost money, but they will require a commitment of your time. It's my job to inform you of the options available, but it's up to you to decide which you want to spend—your money or your time.

Lois joined a dating service and found it was the perfect decision for her lifestyle. A corporate lawyer for a large company in her city, Lois worked long hours, even on weekends. She knew if she didn't hire a dating service to search for a mate, she'd spend the rest of her life single. She promised herself that once she met someone she found to be compatible, she would reduce her hours at work and devote time to building a relationship, but in the meantime she wasn't in a position to spend her own time searching for a mate. The dating service she joined found a compatible match for her within two months. Lois followed through on her commitment, cut back on her work schedule, and is now enjoying her new social life.

No matter what you decide to spend, your money or your time, the important thing is to enjoy yourself! A dating service provides a pleasant, stress-free way to meet people and eventually find your mate. Finding your perfect partner is a numbers game. The more people you meet, the better your chances. Be informed and enjoy the search.

CHAPTER 5: TAKE ACTION

A dating service is a great way to meet people who are a good match for you. Some require more time and less money, while others cost more money but require a minimum, of your time.

If you have a computer, modem, and the appropriate software you might want to give the Internet a try. There are many on-line dating services available on the Internet. If you decide to use one, keep these points in mind:

- Be honest.

- Don't reveal too much about yourself.

- Be wary of fantastic stories. If it sounds too good to be true, it probably is.

- Take precautions when meeting for the first time.

If you can afford it and feel a traditional dating service is something you want to utilize, use the following suggestions:

1. Use the telephone directory to search out and investigate the dating services available to you and decide which one best fits your needs and budget. One excellent way to find a good dating service is through the referral of a satisfied customer. Ask your friends if they, or anyone they know, have found a match through a dating service, and if so which one?

2. As you do your research, refer to these questions:
   - What types of memberships are offered? Long-term, short-term, other?
   - How many years have they been in business?

- How many active members do they have?
- Do they have a customer service department with experienced relationship counselors?
- Will you be having an interview with the person who will do the matching?
- If you meet someone you like, can you put your membership on hold or get a refund?
- What percent of active members are in the age range you prefer?
- Ask for references from past customers.

3. When going on an interview, do something to make yourself memorable.

4. Use the inventories you completed in chapter 3 to insure that you don't forget anything important about yourself or what you want in a potential mate.

Remember, your search for a mate is more important than any job search. Be sure to give yourself every possible opportunity to meet the man or woman of your dreams.

How to Approach Someone You'd Like to Meet

GETTING TO KNOW YOU

Have you ever been in a restaurant or at a party and seen someone you'd really like to meet, but you were afraid to make the first move? Well, you're not alone. The truth is, almost everyone is shy when entering a roomful of strangers. Many people find meeting new people very difficult, but it's really not hard when you know how. In this chapter you will learn some simple, foolproof ways to overcome your anxiety and gain the self-assurance it takes to approach someone new.

The main thing to remember about meeting someone for the first time is that most people want to be met. When you approach someone, you are doing that person a favor. Stop and think about it. How do you feel when someone approaches you at a party and introduces him or herself? Doesn't it make you feel special? Don't you feel relieved when you don't have to make the first move? Isn't it nice to relax and enjoy a conversation with someone who might become a new friend without going out into the crowd and introducing yourself?

Don't make meeting new people more difficult than it is just because you're looking for a mate. To reduce your feelings of nervousness, let go of your expectations. Remember that every time you meet someone you are widening your circle of acquaintances and enhancing your chances of making new friends. Friends provide opportunities for new activities, new ideas, additional emotional support, and even more new friends. Even though the person you befriend at a party, in the line at the supermarket, at a bookstore, or at your son's Little League game may not be the mate you are seeking, he or she could be the person who will introduce you to your mate.

ACT AS IF

Letting go of expectations and thinking of self-introductions as taking the pressure off the other person will be easier for you if you already feel fairly self-confident. But how do you become self-confident if you're a person who is very shy or timid?

Believe it or not, there is an easy way. All you have to do is pretend! That's right. Pretend you have all the confidence in the world. I know it sounds too simple, but this technique works. The mind cannot distinguish between what is real and make-believe. Perception has nothing to do with reality. What we imagine can be as real to us as reality itself. Consequently, the way we act in real life can be determined beforehand by imagining a situation, then imagining the best possible action we could take. This principle is used extensively to train athletes, soldiers, and professionals.

I remember reading an interview with Cary Grant, in which he was asked how he became the suave, debonair man women found irresistible. He answered that he had been an awkward, gangly teenager who used to make-believe he was wonderful, suave, and debonair. Soon he was unable to tell the difference between his make-believe self and his real self.

If you pretend you feel confident long enough, what started as pretense will become real. Act as if you are confident, and you will become confident.

This technique worked for Peter, a graduate of my Light Her Fire class.

Peter was scared to death of women, and especially of rejection. He took my class because he desperately wanted to meet a woman with whom he could have a committed relationship, but he had no skills for approaching or getting acquainted with women.

I asked Peter to pretend for two weeks, thirty minutes each night before he fell asleep, that he was a "ladies' man." He was to think of himself as sexy, handsome, and successful, a man every woman he came in contact with would want to date. In his fantasy, he was to have the phone ringing constantly, with women asking him out and him having to turn them down. He was to say to himself things like, "So many women to choose from, so little time," or "There's only so much of me to spread around. I have to be selective." Then he was to picture himself conversing with the woman of his dreams. He was charming, interesting, funny, and intriguing, and her response to him was extremely positive. Peter spent seven hours tricking his mind, and at the end of that time the change in him was evident.

Soon after he completed the assignment, Peter attended a singles affair. Instead of feeling nervous and insecure when he walked into the roomful of strangers, Peter was surprised by how comfortable he felt. The feelings of self-worth and confidence he had gained from mentally "acting as if" made it much easier for him to approach several women that night.

MAKE YOUR MOVE

There is one very important underlying theme in all of my books, audio programs, and videos: when we fall in love with someone, it is because of the way we feel about ourselves when we are with that person. We all want to be with the person who makes us feel good, whether it's a friend, a family member, or a date. Doesn't it make more sense to let someone know you find him or her attractive than to pretend you aren't interested just because you're afraid of rejection? Making another person feel good about him- or herself is the best way there is to pave the way for romance.

Catherine was attracted to Robert the minute she laid eyes on him at her brother's birthday party. She wanted very much to get to know him. Instead, she avoided him like the plague. She was afraid if she took the initiative she'd appear too aggressive. Catherine was so worried about seeming forward that she didn't even smile at Robert or make eye contact. Because he didn't get signals when he was around her, Robert didn't try to approach Catherine either.

Contrary to popular belief, men need a lot of encouragement before they will risk being rejected. If a woman wants to get to know a man, she must let him know she finds him attractive and is open to being approached. A women who feels she must play hard to get will often be perceived as uninterested or unavailable, and a man will move on to someone more approachable. Had he received a smile or any kind of signal letting him know she was interested, Robert would probably have been open to getting to know Catherine. Because he received no messages from her, Robert assumed Catherine wasn't interested in him.

WHAT'S YOUR EYE Q?

If you don't approach people you find attractive because you haven't a clue how to do it, start watching how other people do it. The next few times you're in a social situation, sit back, relax, and watch other men and women in action. Pay attention to their nonverbal language. Watch how they sit, stand, and gesture. Notice what they do with their eyes and how they smile. Do they ever touch each other? Do they look like they're listening to what the others are saying?

Jerry went to a party and spent most of his time on the couch, observing everyone else in the room. He noticed that most conversations started near the buffet table and realized that food seemed to be a good conversation starter. Jerry watched the chemistry develop between people who smiled and occasionally touched each other. He discovered eye contact was a big factor in bringing people closer. Jerry learned more about how to approach someone by observing others that night than if he had taken a class on flirting.

When you want to meet someone you find attractive, use eye contact to let the person know you're interested. When you catch the person's eye, hold his or her glance for a few seconds—at least long enough to let the person know you've noticed him or her—then look away. Wait a moment, then look at the person again so he or she will know the look was intentional.

Beth did this one day while in a crowded waiting room at a doctor's office. When she sat down, she scanned the waiting area and much to her pleasure she saw a very attractive man. Beth noticed he wasn't wearing a wedding ring and decided then and there she'd like to meet him. She picked up a magazine and began reading it. Every few minutes, she would peer over the top of the magazine to see if she could catch his attention. At one point, their eyes met. Beth held his glance for a moment, then looked away. A brief time later, Beth looked up and caught the man's eye again. The man smiled at her and Beth felt her heart leap. His smile was all she needed for the confidence to take the next step. Beth put the magazine she was reading down, walked over to where the man was sitting and picked out another magazine from the table next to him. When she saw the cover story about the death of Princess Di she made a comment to the man about what a terrible tragedy it was. He agreed, and soon they were engaged in a friendly conversation about the life and death of Princess Diana and the ups and downs of the Royal Family in general.

When using eye contact to get someone's attention, I can't stress enough how important it is to hold the person's glance for at least two to three seconds. If you look away immediately after getting the person's attention, it may be interpreted as disinterest, even if it was shyness that made you avert your gaze. Very shy people are often perceived as unfriendly or standoffish.

Vic learned this lesson the hard way. At a bar one night, Vic noticed a woman who looked interesting. He looked at her several times, but had a hard time getting her attention. Finally, she looked up at the same moment he looked at her. He was so surprised that he quickly looked away. By the time he had the courage to try to get her attention again, she was already engaged in a lively conversation with another man.

SMILE, SMILE, SMILE

Once you have succeeded in making eye contact, you should smile. When you smile, you send the message that you are a happy person, someone who is easy to approach, confident, friendly. If you make eye contact, but don't smile, you'll send the message that you are cold, critical, or aloof.

I know that smiling at someone when you are unsure of the reaction you will get can be scary, but what's the worst that can happen? The target of your smile will look away, instead of returning your smile. You've been rejected. But rejection isn't the worst thing that can happen. Not trying to connect with the person who might be your perfect mate is.

Our intentions come across in the signals we send. If your intention is to send a message that is blatantly sexual rather than one that says, "You look like a person I would like to get to know," your smile might come across as a leer. On the other hand, if your smile is meant to acknowledge that you and the person you are smiling at are both travelers on the path of life, and that perhaps it is time for your paths to cross, your smile will be recognized as one of genuine friendliness.

A smile is much more than a come-on. When you smile at someone, it makes them feel good. Smiling will make you feel better too. When you smile, you release tension and look more attractive. I'm sure you've had the experience of seeing someone's plain-looking face become beautiful when they smile.

Some people find it hard to smile. Perhaps they are self-conscious about having crooked or discolored teeth and feel their smile is actually unattractive. Or, perhaps when they were children they were told to "wipe that smile off your face" so often they've forgotten how to smile.

Marilyn had been brought up in an extremely stern family. Smiling just wasn't something they did very often. Because smiling hadn't been modeled for her as a child, Marilyn had trouble smiling as an adult. In addition, her mouth had been slightly crooked since she was a baby, and people had often commented on it as she was growing up. Their comments had hurt Marilyn, and she avoided smiling rather than show people her "crooked smile."

As an adult, Marilyn longed to smile more easily. She knew people were put off by her serious demeanor and misjudged her as being conceited, which was quite untrue. But she didn't know how to change.

As I told Marilyn, to become comfortable smiling, you have to practice, no matter how difficult it is. At first, practice when you are alone. Use something common in your daily life as a reminder, and every time you see it or hear it, smile. It could be a bell that acts as a reminder. Every time the phone rings, smile. Every time the doorbell rings, smile. When your car chimes to remind you to fasten your seat belt, smile. When you hear a church bell, smile. When you hear a bell on the radio or TV, smile.

If you don't want to use a bell as a reminder, you could use an animal, the sound of water, or anything that is a repetitive element in your life. There are lots of possibilities, but I'm sure you get the picture.

Practice smiling, no matter how you feel. Smile when you are stuck in traffic. Smile as you set the table. Smile when you are cutting carrots. The more you smile, the easier it will become. And as a bonus, the more you smile, the happier you will be.

As smiling becomes a part of your demeanor, smiling at other people will automatically become easier. As you begin to smile at people more, you will notice how a smile attracts people like a magnet. When you smile at them, people will smile back, and the connection you feel will energize you for the rest of the day. Smiling is as important to your well-being as breathing, and once you feel the difference, you'll never want to be without a smile again.

RED LIGHT, GREEN LIGHT

Body language is a very important element in communicating your interest or approachability. We've already talked about the importance of eye contact and smiling. But what are some of the other clues you can send to let a member of the opposite sex know you find them attractive? Your posture, how you position your body in relation to theirs, touch, and facial expression are all ways that can communicate openness or disinterest.

To give you an idea of how all of these factors work together to make a positive or negative impression, let me give you a scenario.

Imagine someone is making a play for your attention, and you find the person completely unacceptable. You have no interest in him or her at all, and in fact, you want the person to leave you alone. What would you do to convey that message, short of telling the person to get lost?

You would probably avoid eye contact. You would look over the person's shoulder at a spot across the room, or you might even turn your head away. You would probably turn your body away slightly and fold your arms across your chest. If the person took a step closer, you would step back. You would frustrate conversation by responding only when necessary, and then with only a yes or no.

Only the densest person would fail to get the message. Your body language has said it all, without a word being spoken.

Your body language can either radiate positive energy and a feeling of openness or can tell people to stay away. Crossed arms can mean, "I'm feeling vulnerable and need to protect myself," or it can mean, "I'm not open to you. Leave me alone."

If you want to be approachable, do not cross your arms. Lift your chin slightly to make eye contact easier, and straighten your shoulders to let people know you are alert and open to meeting them.

By the same token, if someone crosses his or her arms or legs as you approach, or if a person is sitting with his or her head down and shoulders slumped, it probably means the person is unreceptive.

Marlene attended her friend's Christmas party hoping to meet some new people and couldn't understand when no one talked to her. A few weeks later, when her friend showed her pictures from the party, Marlene realized why no one had approached her. The photos showed Marlene slumped in a corner of the couch with her arms folded and chin down. Marlene was shocked to see what a negative impression her posture had given. From that moment on, Marlene made sure to keep her chin up, she kept her arms in an open position, and she smiled and made eye contact whenever she saw someone she was interested in meeting.

JUST DO IT!

No matter how you get someone's attention, sooner or later you have to talk to the person. Smiling, eye contact and body language are great, but they are just a springboard to conversation. The only way you're going to get comfortable meeting new people is to get up from your chair, walk across the room and introduce yourself.

It takes courage to initiate conversation. Almost everyone is afraid of being rejected. To help you deal with the fear of rejection, I want you to stop thinking about yourself! Shift your focus to the other person and concentrate on learning as much as you can about him or her. Of course, you'll want to comment on those things you find particularly interesting or that mesh with your interests and opinions, but being a good listener is the best way to make a connection. Have a few standard phrases or questions you feel comfortable using as conversation starters. If you're at a party, ask the person you want to meet how he or she is acquainted with the host or hostess. If you're waiting for the bus, talk about the weather. If you're in the supermarket, ask for advice or an opinion about something the person has in his or her shopping cart. A simple approach is always best. You don't have to act like a genius or demonstrate your knowledge about current events to impress someone. Showing off or bragging are not attractive qualities. The most attractive people I know are those who are genuine, sincere, and friendly.

Practice meeting new people by talking to everyone. Don't wait to try out an opening phrase or a new approach when you see someone you're attracted to. Practice being friendly wherever you go: at the bus stop, at the library, in line at the movies or the market, in the elevator, at the dentist's office. With enough practice, meeting new people will soon become something you anticipate with pleasure, rather than with a pounding heart and sweaty palms.

In the meantime, if you see someone you want to meet and you're still afraid, feel the fear and say something anyway. Everyone is afraid of being rejected, but you don't have to let your fear rule your life. When you understand that fear and excitement are experienced in the body in the same way, you can use your fear to your advantage. Think about it. When you feel fear, you get butterflies in your stomach, your palms sweat, and your knees knock. Now, how do you feel when you're excited? Exactly the same way. The difference is in your interpretation. So, the next time you see someone you want to meet, feel your butterflies, feel your sweaty palms, feel your knocking knees. But, instead of telling yourself you're afraid, tell yourself you're excited. Remember, your subconscious mind will believe whatever you tell it.

Another method of dealing with fear is to ask yourself, "What's the worst that can happen?" Draw a worst-case scenario and use it as the push you need to go ahead with whatever it is that frightens you. Then, feel the fear and do it anyway.

Adam stood by the buffet table at a singles' dance feeling as if his feet were stuck in cement. The woman he wanted so much to talk to was just five feet away from him conversing with another woman. Instead of putting one foot in front of the other and walking up to her, he befriended the chicken wings while he practiced saying "hello" over and over in his head. Once he finally felt courageous enough to approach her, he looked up and was heartbroken to see the woman dancing with another man.

Adam let his fear keep him from meeting a woman he found very attractive. If he had only been able to act in spite of his fear, or transform it into excitement, his evening could have ended quite differently.

After the first few times, speaking to someone new will become much easier and you'll begin to understand something else about human nature. Just as you'll learn that when you begin smiling at strangers, they'll smile back, you'll find that you tend to get back verbally what you give out. When you say "Hi" to someone, you'll usually get a "Hi" in return. If you say "Hello," the person will respond with "Hello." If you say "Hi, my name is John," the response will be, "Hi, my name is Ellen."

When you first meet someone either say "Hello" and introduce yourself immediately, or ask the person a question that will initiate conversation. Once the conversation is under way, introduce yourself. Either way, when you give the person your name, take the opportunity to shake hands. Give him or her a firm, friendly handshake, but not so firm that you crush the person's hand. A wonderful way to let someone know how interested you are is to hold his or her hand in both of yours when you shake. This two-handed shake is a warm, non-threatening way to touch someone you've just met.

One of the best ways to show you are interested in someone is to remember his or her name when you are introduced. We all think the sound of our name is the sweetest sound we've ever heard. When you call a person by name, he or she feels flattered and automatically feels as though you are a friend.

If you have problems remembering names there are entire courses and books devoted to developing a better memory. These courses teach you tricks to enhance your memory, such as using a mental image or wordplay to remember a name. For example, if a person's name is Val, think of him as "Val, the valiant." If her name is Cindy, think of her as "Cindy-rella." If his name is Steve, picture a stevedore on a dock, loading cargo onto a ship.

Another trick to help you remember someone's name, is to repeat it as soon as you hear it. For instance, when someone says, "My name is Shelly," you can immediately say, "It's nice to meet you, Shelly." Repeat the person's name a few more times during the conversation. Besides helping you to remember it, repeating a person's name will please him or her and make the person feel special.

Gordon learned to play the name game, but not until he'd blundered a few times. He met a woman at a wedding reception that he found extremely attractive. She introduced herself as Madeline. Instead of repeating her name right away, Gordon trusted his memory. A few minutes into their conversation, he called her Melanie and she politely corrected him. A little later, Gordon introduced Madeline to a friend and called her Melanie again. This time, she was not so polite. Within seconds, she excused herself. He didn't see her the rest of the evening.

Once you've broken the ice, you'll know very soon whether or not the conversation is going to continue, but for the conversation to go somewhere, it has to start in the first place.

Raymond never would have known he and Deborah had so much to talk about if he hadn't gone beyond making eye contact and waving to her. Raymond caught Deborah's attention at a singles event at his church by flashing a smile and tipping his baseball cap. Once he got her attention, he didn't know what to do with it. He mouthed the words "Hi" from across the room and raised his eyebrows a couple times to let her know he was interested. Deborah smiled back at him, so Raymond took the next step and walked over to her, shook her hand, and introduced himself. They spent the next two hours talking to each other.

THE CONVERSATION

Do you know what Jay Leno, David Letterman, and Conan O'Brian have in common? They are all experts at bringing out the best in people. No matter how dull, how boring, or how uncomfortable their guests may be, these late-night talk show hosts are able to conduct an interview that makes them entertaining and interesting. What's their secret? During the interview, they focus on the guest, keeping the conversation light and positive, and asking open-ended questions to encourage active participation. If talking to another person is difficult for you, you might pick up some tips on the art of conversation by watching these talented men as they turn a nine-year-old spelling bee champion or a seventy-nine-year-old Senior Olympics competitor into an interesting guest.

If you choose to open a conversation with someone you've just met by asking a question, make sure it's an open-ended question instead of one that can be answered with a yes or no. For instance, "What do you think about the band?" will stimulate conversation, while, "Do you like the band?" will elicit a yes or no and lead to a deadend.

Once you've gotten past the introductions, make sure your first comment is light and positive. Be prepared to laugh easily. You certainly don't want to force a laugh, but if you have an easygoing, casual attitude, laughter will come naturally. When you first meet someone, avoid heavy topics like religion or politics. Keep your conversation light-hearted and enthusiastic. Stay away from complaining and sarcasm. Negative comments will make a bad impression.

Fred was shocked when a woman he was talking with at a party abruptly excused herself and walked away. He turned to his friend and said he couldn't understand why she would walk away like that. Fred's friend told him the reason she walked away was probably because she got tired of hearing about his herniated disc. Fred didn't realize it, but he had spent the first five minutes of the conversation telling the woman about his back problems. The woman was at the party to have fun and meet people, not to hear Fred's medical history.

A good way to keep your conversation upbeat is to compliment the other person. You wouldn't have been attracted to them if you hadn't seen something appealing to begin with, so tell them about it. When giving a compliment, use your imagination and be specific. For example, if you were to comment on a man's shirt, simply saying, "That's a nice shirt," you'd probably make his day. But if you take it one step further and say, "That's a great shirt. It brings out the color of your eyes. Where did you get it?" it will have a much greater impact, and it will also lead to further conversation. The first example will make someone feel good, but the second one shows that you're paying more attention and noticing something special about him or her. Whatever you do, avoid telling someone he or she looks nice. "Nice" is a meaningless word that sounds lifeless when you say it.

Shannon walked into her friend's birthday party wearing a pair of long, dangling earrings she had designed and made herself. It didn't take long for Nathan to notice Shannon and her earrings. He walked up to her and instead of saying, "I like your earrings," he said, "Wow, what unusual earrings. They look great with your short haircut." Shannon talked to no one but Nathan the entire evening.

Another way to keep a conversation positive and full of energy is to tell a good story. Story telling is a wonderful way to keep a conversation alive and at the same time show off your sense of humor or your flair for drama. Remember to share the stage with the other person, though. Stories are great as long as they don't turn into monologues or one-person shows.

Sally and Dean met at a college graduation party and began talking about how bad the food was in their dormitory.

They had a fabulous time as they swapped stories about mystery meat and mashed potatoes that could be used for glue. The key to their successful discussion was that they took turns telling stories. Neither one of them monopolized the conversation.

REACH OUT AND TOUCH SOMEONE

How you position yourself in relation to the person you're talking to can have an effect on the impression you give. When talking with someone, it's important to face him or her. If you're sitting beside someone, make sure you turn to look at the person. Don't be afraid to get a little closer. Don't get so close that you're breathing down the person's neck, but don't leave too much distance either.

Once you feel comfortable with the distance between yourself and the other person, look for an opportunity to touch him or her. One way to do this is to listen carefully to what the person is saying. When something is said that you agree with, touch his or her arm lightly and say, "I know what you mean," or "I feel the same way." A gentle touch like this is a wonderful way to make a connection and let someone know that you really like being with him or her.

As you begin your conversation, pay attention to how much you're talking. If you feel the conversation is lopsided and you're doing most of the talking, stop! While your input is important, make sure you do your share of listening as well.

Another way to indicate you really like someone is to show the person a particular courtesy or kindness. Going out of your way for someone you find attractive is a sure way to make a good impression. You can open a door, pull up a chair, or offer to get something from the bar or buffet table. Help someone on or off with his or her coat, offer to carry something for the person, or offer to walk a woman to her car. In short, make someone's life a little easier. The person will remember your kindness, and most importantly, he or she will remember you!

BE A GOOD LISTENER

Very few people are good listeners. Most people are so intent on making a good impression that, instead of listening when another person speaks, they are thinking about what they are going to say next. A good listener is able to suspend his or her own thoughts and feelings in order to hear what the other person is saying. When you listen well, you listen with more than your ears, you listen with your mind and your heart as well. And as you listen, you begin to see things from another point of view. Good listening promotes closeness and understanding. Be a good listener, and you will have a new friend in no time.

A good way to show someone you're listening to what he or she is saying is to ask specific questions. Ask someone to clarify or describe in more detail something he or she is talking about to show that you're really listening.

Another way is to mirror what has just been said. For example, when the person you are talking to says, "I'm really excited about my upcoming trip to Europe," you say, "I can tell that you are really looking forward to it."

Chelsey and Mort met and started talking while visiting an art gallery. Chelsey told Mort how much she enjoyed a drawing class she was taking and mentioned that she found it hardest to draw figures. Mort wanted her to know he was interested in what she was saying so he asked her to explain more about why drawing figures was so difficult. Besides asking specific questions, he used body language to show Chelsey he was interested in what she was saying by putting his hand under his chin and leaning forward a little as they sat together on a bench in the gallery.

When talking with someone, a certain amount of silence is okay. When the other person says something, it's not necessary to jump right in with a response. Sit with the silence for a few seconds and reflect before you reply. Taking time to think about what has been said is another way to show that you're listening. If the pause turns into a lull in the conversation, you can always go back to what you were talking about before.

You may think this all sounds very contrived and manipulative, but it really isn't. What I am actually suggesting in each instance is that you concentrate on really *being* with the person you're talking to. Being a good listener is a skill that will not only help you in beginning a relationship with someone you're attracted to, it will help make you a desirable person to be with in any situation. People who are liked know how to make other people feel special and important by listening intently to what they say.

THAT'S WHAT FRIENDS ARE FOR

Another strategy for easing the way when meeting new people is to bring a friend along. Frequently, a friend will find it easier to strike up a conversation with the person you're interested in than you do.

Before you put such a plan into action, you and your friend need to agree on certain things. Make sure your friend understands ahead of time that he or she is to be the opening act, but that you are to be the main attraction. Make it clear that, once the conversation is in full swing and you are a part of it, your friend should step out of the picture, with a plausible excuse. You can do the same thing for your friend when the time comes.

Before going to a singles meeting at their church, Jodie and Maureen agreed that if one of them saw someone they wanted to meet, the other would stay close. They would help the other get the conversation going, and then quietly drop out of the picture.

During the evening, Jodie saw a man who interested her and both Jodie and Maureen approached him. They introduced themselves and began talking about the speaker for the meeting. Whenever there was a lull in the conversation, Maureen helped out by bringing up another subject. Once Jodie and Hank started talking about downhill skiing, something they had in common, Maureen excused herself to go talk to another friend.

LOCATION, LOCATION, LOCATION

There's a truism in the real estate business that the three most important factors to consider in buying property are: location, location, location. I think the same thing could be said for how to make yourself approachable. If you sit in a booth at a restaurant instead of at the counter, if you hide at a corner table instead of sitting right next to the dance floor, or if you always sit next to a member of the same sex on the bus, you make it much more difficult for someone to approach you. Put yourself within reach! When you're at a party, stay where the people are. You can't hide out in the den and expect to meet anyone when everyone else is in the living room. If you're at a night-club, you'll be a lot more accessible if you sit at the bar, instead of at a table that requires someone to walk through an obstacle course just to get to you.

If you see someone interesting across the room from you, find an excuse to walk by him or her. Even though there is a more direct route to the restroom, for example, take the long way, make eye contact, and flash a smile as you pass by. Repeat the same routine on the way back. If you get a good response, this might be the perfect time to ask for a dance.

MAY I HAVE THIS DANCE?

Asking someone to dance is a great way to let someone know you find him or her attractive. It's true that dancing and talking at the same time can be difficult, but you don't have to wait until the dance is over to have a conversation. Sometimes it's hard to hear over music or to talk and move your feet at the same time, so instead of worrying about making small talk, let your body do the talking.

When you're dancing with someone you like, make eye contact. Once you decide how close you want to get to the person, there are a lot of things you can do to indicate your interest. If you're a man, you can draw your partner a little closer, unless you sense she's not comfortable being that close. If you're a woman, you can put your hand on your partner's back, rather than resting it on his shoulder. You can squeeze your partner's hand or gently caress his or her back. If you're fast dancing, make a lot of eye contact with your partner. Looking around the room as you're dancing sends the message that you feel uncomfortable or that you'd rather be doing something else.

There are all kinds of subtle moves you can make to tell your partner you like him or her. The next time you're somewhere where there's dancing, watch the people on the dance floor. Most of them aren't saying a word to each other, but messages are flying back and forth loud and clear.

Simon and Claire saw each other from across the room at a wedding reception. Their eyes locked, but they were both afraid to make the first move. When the music started, Simon walked over to Claire and asked her to dance. Claire followed Simon onto the dance floor. During the five minutes they fast danced together, although no words were spoken, they had a very meaningful conversation. They rarely lost eye contact and smiled at each other the entire time they danced. When the music ended, they sat down and spent the next three hours talking. By dancing first they were able to avoid the awkward first minutes of introductions.

Another way to approach someone for the first time is to buy the person a drink. When the person you're interested in orders, watch carefully to see what he or she is drinking. If you can't figure it out by watching, ask the waitress and have her let the person know who bought the drink. If the person you're interested in is with a friend, it would be a nice gesture to buy the friend a drink also. Once the drink is delivered, watch for the person to wave or acknowledge you, but even if he or she doesn't, go over and introduce yourself. If he or she is with another person, introduce yourself to the friend as well. Although you may only want to have a conversation with the person you're interested in, don't exclude the person's friend from the conversation.

Drew was at a neighborhood bar one evening and noticed two women sitting at a nearby table. One woman in particular caught his attention. He noticed both women had soft drinks. Drew asked the waitress what the women were drinking and had her deliver another round. He asked the waitress to tell them their drinks were with his compliments and point him out.

When the drinks were delivered, the women looked surprised and pleased as they waved and mouthed, "Thank you." Drew immediately got up and walked over to their table. He introduced himself to both women and asked if he could join them. Although Drew was only attracted to one of the women, he made sure he didn't ignore her friend. When it came time to leave, he suggested they all swap business cards. The next week he called the woman he had been attracted to and they began dating. Later, Marie told Drew how much it had impressed her that he had been so attentive to both her and her friend.

'TIL WE MEET AGAIN

You can talk to someone you're interested in all night long, but what do you do when it's time to leave? Like Drew, you could swap business cards and agree to stay in touch. The problem is that sometimes the next day your confidence fades and you never make a follow-up call. The best way to ensure that you'll see the person again is to set up another meeting before you go your separate ways. You can wait for the other person to suggest another time to get together, but if he or she doesn't, make sure you do. Why wait? You've just spent a concentrated amount of time together. There's chemistry flowing between the two of you, so keep it going. Ride the wave while it's still high. You can always agree to touch base with each other to confirm your plans, but at least make tentative ones before you leave.

Even though every person you're attracted to might not be mate material, don't think you've wasted your time if he or she doesn't turn out to be the man or woman of your dreams. It's important to give as much positive energy as you can to each person you meet in your quest for a mate. Remember, meeting people is like going on a job interview. Every time you do it, you get better at it until one day you land the job of your dreams. It's the same way with relationships. Approach, approach, approach. Keep at it until it becomes as easy as talking to your best friend. The day you meet the love of your life, your practice and experience will have been well worth it!

CHAPTER 6: TAKE ACTION

Letting go of expectations and feeling self-confident are keys to approaching new people. Use your journal to work on ways to gain confidence and perfect your approach.

1. If approaching someone you are interested in makes you break out in a cold sweat, use the "act as if" technique to imagine yourself introducing yourself to new people effortlessly. Use the technique faithfully every day, for two weeks, for thirty minutes each day, and watch as your fantasy becomes reality.

2. Practice smiling. Begin by smiling when you are alone, and gradually work up to smiling at strangers. Make a note of the responses you get.

3. Be aware of your body language. Make a special effort to maintain an open body position, with your chin up and your arms uncrossed.

4. In your journal, write down as many opening lines as you can think of that fit your personality and your lifestyle. Remember to keep them upbeat and positive.

5. Practice these openings by approaching new people everywhere you go. Keep notes in your journal about your experience as you practice, practice, practice.

6. Find ways to be helpful and courteous to other people as you go about your daily life. By making this a part of your regular routine, it will become second nature to you and you won't have to think about it when you want to show kindness to someone you're attracted to.

7. Enhance your conversation skills by developing the habit of asking open-ended questions. Instead of asking, "Do you like the band?" ask, "What do you think about the band?"

8. When you notice something you like about a person, tell him or her.

9. Practice being a good listener with everyone you meet.

Remember, people want to be met. Make someone's day by making the first move, and you'll be well on your way to meeting the man or woman of your dreams.

First Dates

Whether it happens when you're sixteen or sixty, going on a first date is one of the best ways I know of to get your adrenaline flowing and your heart pumping. Even if you've talked to your prospective date several times on the phone and feel you know that person, there's something about the first meeting that makes your heart pound, your palms sweat, and your mouth go dry.

The anticipation of wanting to meet the right person combined with the fear of meeting the wrong person, makes for a situation filled with anxiety. But keep in mind that first dates are just that—first dates. Nothing is etched in stone. There's no contract, no lifelong commitment.

Remember, life is an adventure. First dates can be an exciting part of that adventure. Even if your first date turns

out to be your last date, it is always an opportunity to learn—
about another person, and about yourself.

Much of the success of a first date depends on how well planned
it is. I can't stress enough that on a first date you should *always*
meet in a public place. I don't care if your grandmother set you
up with a blind date, or if you've talked to your potential date
on the phone for hours and feel as if you're old friends, it is
much safer to meet at a coffee shop or restaurant than to allow
your date to pick you up or to go to his or her home.

Pick a place with an atmosphere that feels good to you. It
should be neither too loud, nor too quiet. If cost is a considera-
tion, pick something that is in the moderate price range. Many
people are comfortable meeting in generic-type coffee shops.
While they may lack ambiance, they have many advantages.
They are always conveniently located, are often open 24 hours
a day so that you can meet for breakfast, lunch, afternoon
snack, or dinner, are modestly priced, are well lit, and there are
people in and out at any hour. Remember, your first date is a
continuation of the interview process. Romantic, candlelight
dinners are not appropriate at this stage of the game.

If possible, you should make the meeting place close to
where you live. I realize this is difficult in a large, sprawling
city, but the less time you have to spend meeting people, the
more people you can meet. Decide how much time you're
willing to spend commuting and stick to your decision. That
way you'll avoid feeling resentful about the time spent if the
date doesn't work out.

Second, plan the date so if it doesn't go well, you can leave. Having your own transportation and being able to leave easily at any time will help you feel more comfortable when meeting new people. It's always a good idea for first dates to be short rather than long. Keeping it short will help you stay focused on the interview process and will make it more comfortable to end the date if it isn't going smoothly. If you've committed yourself to an entire evening, or you don't have a way to get home on your own, you could end up feeling like a prisoner. Usually, you won't find it necessary to leave early, but there's always the possibility that you just can't stand to spend another minute with this person. In that case, having your own transportation represents freedom.

Third, be specific about where you will meet. Avoid confusion by using some type of obvious landmark. Agreeing to meet at a shopping center, a theater, or a park is much too general. It's a good idea to scope out possible meeting places and have a list at hand before beginning to make dates. If you have addresses, phone numbers, and directions available, it will make the planning go more smoothly and help you sidestep unpleasant misunderstandings.

Lisa and Gerald met through a personal ad. Their first phone conversation went well and they decided to meet for lunch at a food court in a nearby shopping mall. The only problem was, they didn't agree on a specific place to meet. When they arrived, the mall was jam-packed with people, all on their lunch hour. Lisa and Gerald spent twenty minutes roaming around the food court looking for each other. Frustrated and hungry, each of them got in line at a different fast food restaurant, sat down at a table, and ate lunch alone.

When they connected by phone that evening, Lisa and Gerald discovered they were almost in the same place at the same time, but neither one knew it because they hadn't been specific enough about where to meet.

If you've never met, describe yourself to your date, and get a description of him or her as well. Hair color, hair style, height, mustache, and so on are starting points, but may be too general for you to confidently walk up and introduce yourself. Try to wear or carry something that will make you easy to identify. In the movie, "You've Got Mail," Meg Ryan carried a book with a flower in it to help Tom Hanks identify her at the restaurant where they agreed to meet.

MOVIE MADNESS

For your first date, it's a good idea to stay away from very noisy places. You'll want to be somewhere where you can have a conversation without straining to hear or having to yell over the noise of the crowd.

I also advise against going to a movie on your first date. The movies may have been a safe bet when you were in high school, but you are on a search for a mate. You've invested time and money in meeting this person. Don't waste it sitting in a movie theater where you can't interact or even get a good look at each other.

Ruth and Daryl decided to see a movie for their first date. They met under the marquee, made small talk for a couple of minutes while they got their popcorn, and then said nothing to each other for two hours. When they walked out of the movie theater, they tried to make conversation, but it was very difficult. They talked about the movie a little on the way to their cars, but they never really connected. Their date ended after the movie, and so did their relationship.

If you are too uncomfortable with the idea of sitting in a cafe for an hour and a half or two hours, and feel you need some form of entertainment to take the pressure off, there are many other things you can do where you'll be entertained and still able to talk and get to know each other. A sporting event where you can at least talk about the action and cheer your team is a better choice than a movie. Go bowling, play miniature golf, visit a museum or a public garden. All these activities are fun and can help keep a conversation flowing.

First dates don't have to involve food. If you're the active type, you could take a walk in a scenic, but well-populated area, or go rollerblading or bike-riding instead. But eating together somehow makes people feel connected, so you might want to talk over a cup of coffee or an ice cream cone afterwards.

Your first date has a better chance of being successful if you and your date are both comfortable with the meeting place and the activity. If your date suggests an idea or place that you aren't agreeable to, say so. If you accept a date knowing you won't be comfortable, the date is doomed before it even begins.

After meeting briefly at a party, Pamela and Eric decided they wanted to see each other again. Pamela was going to a family reunion the following weekend, and invited Eric to come. Eric smiled and said he would like to go, but thought to himself that a family reunion was the last place he'd want to be for a first date. He went anyway and was extremely uncomfortable the entire time. He didn't know anyone at the reunion and felt as if he were on display for Pamela's family. Their first date was such an unpleasant experience that Eric never called Pamela again.

If you've been too passive or submissive in your past relationships, planning your first date is a good place to begin to assert yourself and set boundaries. When Ryan suggested to Vivian that they meet at a particular pub in their city, she was immediately honest with him about her discomfort. She told him she had been to that pub before and hadn't felt very safe parking in the area. Ryan said he could understand why she wouldn't want to meet there and asked if she had any other ideas. Vivian suggested a restaurant in a different neighborhood, and Ryan agreed to it. Vivian felt good about being able to assert herself, and she liked Ryan's easy acceptance of her alternative suggestion. The date was off to a good start.

TEA FOR TWO

Although evening may seem like the most obvious time to have a first date, don't rule out other times of the day. Breakfast and lunch dates are a good alternative and since each of you will probably have other plans for the rest of the day, they make ending the date easier.

Helen and Earl decided to meet at an exclusive downtown hotel for afternoon tea. It was something Helen had always wanted to do, Earl agreed that it sounded like an excellent idea and they had a wonderful time sitting by the fire, listening to the soft sounds of a harp and chatting as they sipped their favorite tea and selected delectable desserts served on a silver platter.

After you've agreed on where and when to have your first date, it's time to close your conversation. Exchanging phone numbers is a good idea, in case either of you has a change of plans and can't make the date. I know there may be a slight risk involved in giving your phone number to someone you've never met, and you shouldn't do it if you don't feel comfortable, but I haven't figured out another way to connect if it should become necessary.

Henry and Sophia met at a college alumni dinner and had a great time together. They agreed to see each other again and planned a first date for the following week. Unfortunately, they forgot to exchange phone numbers. The evening of their date, Henry had a family emergency and couldn't meet Sophia. He tried getting her phone number through information, but it was unlisted. He felt badly, but he couldn't meet her.

The next year, Henry and Sophia saw each other again at the alumni dinner. Still angry because she had been stood up by him, Sophia avoided meeting Henry's eyes. Henry finally was able to connect with Sophia and he apologized profusely for standing her up. Henry explained everything, and Sophia realized that he had never intended to hurt her. This time they exchanged phone numbers right away, and they finally had their first date a year later than originally intended. A little late, maybe, but better late than never—since they've been married now for several years.

THE DRESS CODE IS COMFORTABLE

It's important to look your best when you go out on your date, but it's even more important to feel comfortable in whatever you are wearing. Remember, you want your first date to be a positive experience. The last thing you want is to be tugging at a dress that's too tight or pulling at your collar because your shirt has too much starch. You've put a lot of effort into picking a comfortable place and time to meet. What you wear shouldn't be any less comfortable.

Harry went out and bought a new sweater for his first date with Marsha. When he tried it on in the store, it fit perfectly and looked terrific on him. It was only a few minutes into the date that Harry began to itch. He tried to hide his discomfort from Marsha, but all he could think about was how much he wanted to scratch himself. Unfortunately, Marsha thought Harry's distraction came from a lack of interest in what she was saying. Finally, Marsha asked Harry if she was boring him. When he realized that he was making a bad impression, he explained that his new sweater was driving him crazy. If Marsha hadn't confronted Harry on his behavior, she would never have known that his distraction had nothing to do with her.

As you prepare to start dating, you need to think how you will handle things when it comes time to pay the check. It doesn't matter whether you are a man or a woman, there are no hard and fast rules, only what is comfortable for you. A lot depends on who suggests the place you are meeting and what type of place it is. As you make plans for your first date, cost should be considered in the equation. Remember, you will be going out on a lot of first dates, often as many as two or three a week, which could quickly put a strain on your pocketbook. If your prospective date suggests an expensive dinner, and you feel that it is not within your budget, you should say something about it at the outset. You might say something like,

"I've heard wonderful things about (such and such). I'm sure it's very nice, but I'd really be more comfortable with something a little less elegant." If your date offers to pay for it, and you're comfortable with that, then let them do so. If you want to pay your half of the bill, then be assertive and say so and insist on going somewhere you can afford. Whatever the circumstances, just make sure you do what you are comfortable with rather than doing something you don't want to.

THE ART OF CONVERSATION

During your first date, give yourselves plenty of time to interact with each other. The purpose of a first date is not romance, it is discovery. Ideally, you will have an opportunity to learn about each other in a comfortable setting and your conversation will be a balanced give and take of information. At the same time, your face-to-face meeting will offer you the opportunity to see if there is any chemistry between the two of you.

If you are a talker, you'll probably feel most comfortable with a good listener. But it's still important to find out what your date is all about and what they have to say.

On their first date, Judith and Matthew had dinner together, and Judith listened while Matthew talked for two hours. By the time their date was over, Judith had heard all about the new product line Matthew was selling for his company but knew little else about him. Although Matthew thought he would impress Judith with his knowledge, Judith found his monologue self-centered. Every once in a while, Judith would try to interject a comment. Matthew would listen just long enough for Judith to get her last word out, then he'd start talking again.

Judith was very polite throughout the dinner and nodded and smiled, but she couldn't wait until the evening was over.

Besides not monopolizing the conversation, it's best to keep your conversation positive. Certain topics are guaranteed to act as ice-makers instead of ice-breakers. As tempting as it is to bare your soul to someone who appears to be a good listener, don't talk about what was wrong with your ex-wife, how much you hate your job, your health problems, your difficult teenager, or your overdrawn checking account. Unless, of course, you never want to see the person again.

Even if you're more of a talker than the other person, for your own sake it's important to slow down and encourage your date to talk by asking open-ended questions. Saying "Tell me what brought you to this city?" or "What is it about your job that you like the most?" will let your date know you care about what they have to say and will give you the opportunity to do what it is you set out to do on a first date—get acquainted!

If you tend to be on the quiet side, you'll probably be most comfortable with a good talker, but it's still important to make sure you contribute to the conversation. Your date wants to know you, and they want to know you are interested in them. If you answer questions with a one-word reply, or don't ask any questions of your own, you will probably be perceived as bored, disinterested, or both.

Danny was very shy and found making conversation difficult. When he went on his first date with Arlene, he listened carefully to all she said, but made very little comment. If Arlene asked him a question, Danny would answer in as few words as possible, often responding with just yes or no. After awhile, Arlene began to think that Danny was bored. Trying hard to find a subject that would draw Danny out, Arlene asked him if he had ever been skiing. When Danny answered yes but didn't say anything else, Arlene gave up. Arlene had given Danny a perfect opportunity to make conversation. He could have told Arlene where he had been skiing, whether he preferred down-hill or cross-country skiing, what his level of expertise was, or even asked her about her skiing experiences, but he didn't pick up the ball when it was tossed to him. Whenever your date asks a question, make sure you elaborate with a story so the other person can get to know you better.

I'm not saying you should change the way you are. It's important for you to be comfortable with yourself, just as you are. I just want you to be aware that on your first date it's important to let the other person know you care about them if you ever want to see them again. So, if you're a great talker, be aware you need to ask some questions to draw the other person into the conversation. If you're a good listener, you need to do some talking to let the other person know you're interested.

CELEBRATE THE DIFFERENCES

In all of my tape programs and books, I talk about how oppo-sites attract. We are drawn to someone who has strengths, weaknesses, and a personality opposite to ours. If, while on your first date, you notice your partner has several qualities completely opposite from yours, don't worry. If you feel com-fortable and like each other, give yourselves a chance at a rela-tionship by having a second date. Those qualities that are opposite to yours often complement your personality and make for a wonderfully cohesive and balanced relationship. Unfortunately, many people focus so much on the differences that they don't realize that it's the differences that make the relationship work!

When Valerie and Gregory went on their first date, it didn't take them long to notice the differences in their personalities. Valerie was outgoing and highly energetic, while Gregory's personality was much more low-key. Gregory had never been much of a talker, but with Valerie he found himself contributing to the conversation more than he normally did. She had a way of drawing him into the conversation. At the same time, Valerie felt really listened to by Gregory, who was a born listener. Valerie and Gregory's opposite qualities complemented each other like two pieces of a puzzle that fit together perfectly.

OVERCOMING ANXIETY

First dates are often anxiety-ridden. If you have never met before, your nervousness may affect your time together. Blind dates can be especially trying. If you're going on a blind date, it's probably because some well-meaning friend or relative has set you up with someone they know. Between being nervous about meeting the other person and feeling a little pressured to hit it off because you've been set up by a friend or relative, you may not put your best foot forward.

The best way to let go of anxiety is to let go of expectations. You and your date are not on trial, you're on an adventure of discovery. Instead of worrying about whether you'll like each other or have anything in common, relax and enjoy the process. Remember, even if your date doesn't turn out to be your perfect mate, you can still have a good time. Try to channel your nervous energy into excitement. And, don't forget to breathe. This may sound silly but many people actually hold their breath when they are nervous or tense.

Laurie was extremely nervous about her first date with Jim. She wanted so much to make a good impression that she got a manicure, had her hair done, and even had her teeth cleaned in anticipation of their date. She hadn't slept well for the three nights preceding their date and had hardly been able to eat for the previous 24 hours. During their dinner date, Laurie began to feel very dizzy. She didn't know whether it was from fatigue or hunger, but halfway through the appetizer course, Laurie had to excuse herself to go to the restroom. Once she was safely alone, she took several slow, deep breaths and began to feel better immediately. Without realizing it, Laurie had been holding her breath a lot. As soon as she began breathing, her dizziness went away and her nervousness subsided as well.

Jim and Laurie now laugh about Laurie's tendency to hold her breath when she gets nervous and how Jim had to whisper, "Breathe, Laurie, breathe!" as they stood at the altar on their wedding day.

SECOND CHANCES

Everybody goes through the first date jitters. A person may blush, stutter, and fumble. But unless your date is doing something totally unacceptable, give him or her a chance to feel comfortable, and hopefully, he or she will do the same for you.

Bonnie and Gary's first date was arranged by Gary's brother, who was Bonnie's friend. Gary had never gone on a blind date before, but agreed to it because he knew it would make his brother happy.

Gary was so nervous when he met Bonnie in the restaurant lobby, he shook her hand and said, "Hi. I'm Larry. I mean Gary." During dinner, Gary dropped his napkin under the table and flipped a water chestnut onto Bonnie's blouse while attempting to use his chopsticks.

Bonnie could have become annoyed with Gary's nervousness and written him off, but she saw past Gary's social blunders and decided to give their relationship another chance. They went out again the following week and had a fabulous time. Each time they went on a date, Gary felt less and less nervous. The only time he got as nervous as on their first date was on their wedding day.

Some of you may believe you have to hear bells or see fireworks to know you've met your perfect mate. This is absolutely not true. When love at first sight does happen and the subsequent relationship works out, it's sheer luck. Sometimes people do fall in love at first sight, but more often it's only lust at first sight. Chemistry is important, but sometimes sparks don't start to fly until you've gotten to know someone better. If you only give a person one chance to ring your bell, you could be missing out on meeting the perfect person for you. I firmly believe in giving a person a second chance. Just because you don't fall head over heels in love with someone on the first date is no reason not to see that person again. It's not always easy to know immediately whether someone is a good match for you.

Lisa was performing in a 1940s musical revue at a theater in her city when she met Cliff. Her part in the show was to get audience members to participate by asking them to dance. One night, the emcee asked Lisa to go out into the audience and dance with Cliff, a friend of his who was feeling low because he had just been laid off. Lisa peeked out from backstage to get a glimpse of Cliff and was immediately turned off. "No way," she said. "This guy looks too depressed." After some coaxing from the emcee, Lisa agreed.

As she approached him, she kept telling herself that it wouldn't kill her to dance one dance with this guy. Lisa walked up to Cliff, smiled, and invited him to dance with her. With a rather glum expression, Cliff accepted. They walked to the dance floor and began to jitterbug. Within seconds, Lisa was having the time of her life. Cliff was the best dancer she had danced with in the year and a half the show had been running.

They talked a little after the show, and when Cliff asked Lisa to go out with him, she wasn't quite sure why, but she agreed to a date. He wasn't really her type. She was usually attracted to big, well-built men and Cliff was on the thin side, and he certainly did seem to be depressed, but something told her she should give him a chance.

The next week they went on a date, the first of many. Thinking back on it, Lisa was so thankful she didn't let her first impression of Cliff affect her decision to date him. The second chance she gave Cliff opened her eyes and her heart to the wonderful man she's married to today.

There are plenty of clues that can help you know whether this person is someone you want to see again, even if the chemistry between you wasn't so electric it set the sparks flying.

Were you comfortable? Did you have fun and laugh a lot? Did you feel listened to? Cared about? Were you able to express your ideas? Were you able to relax? Did your date seem to be optimistic and upbeat? If you can answer yes to most of these questions, not going on a second date would be foolish.

LISTEN TO YOUR INTUITION

If, on the other hand, you feel a strong attraction and are very excited about your date, be careful not to get so mesmerized by someone's smile or by your own fantasies of what your date is like, that you ignore the obvious. Pay attention to everything about the person you're with. If your date says or does something that is unacceptable to you, or you sense there may be trouble in the future, you certainly don't have to go on a second date with the person.

When Patricia met Gene at a friend's holiday party, she was attracted to him because of his good looks and great smile. That same smile seemed to take her breath away and almost hypnotized her on their first date. Every time Gene would flash her a smile, Patricia's heart would leap.

About halfway into their dinner, Patricia noticed she wasn't the only one Gene was flashing a smile at. By the end of their dinner, it became obvious to Patricia that Gene was flirting with a woman sitting at a nearby table. Although she remained polite for the rest of their date, she decided then and there not to give Gene a second chance.

If Patricia had allowed herself to be totally captivated by Gene's smile and charm, she might have rationalized his flirting with the other woman as no big deal. Instead she listened to her intuition. She felt sure that Gene's flirting on their first date was probably a warning of things to come and his behavior was unacceptable to her. Under the circumstances, a second date was out of the question.

Don't make the mistake of continuing to date someone who isn't right for you. This is exactly how people become involved in unhappy relationships. Usually, at the point when a person admits that the relationship they've been involved in for six months, a year, or even longer isn't working, they realize that they knew it wasn't right for them from the very beginning, but they ignored all the danger signs and started a relationship anyway. Loneliness, the desire to have a date for social events, or neediness can lead a person to keep dating someone in spite of their gut-level knowledge that this is not the right person for them.

Besides looking for clues that indicate you should give your date a second chance, be aware of clear signs that you shouldn't. Ignoring these signs can only lead to heartache later. When your date tells you something negative about him- or herself, believe it. If the person says something like, "I've got no patience," "I never intend to get married again," "My mother runs my life," "I never miss a football game on television," "I'm not interested in having children," or "My career is the most important thing in my life," you are getting accurate feedback about what you can expect from this person in the future. If you hear something you know is unacceptable to you, don't go for a second date, no matter how strong the chemistry is. Completing your "personal inventory" and your "ideal mate inventory" are excellent ways to stay focused on what's right for you and not be led astray by chemistry, loneliness, or neediness.

Lack of self-esteem is another reason people will date the wrong person. Some people think so little of themselves that they grab onto the first person that shows an interest in them, even if that person isn't right for them. Because they're afraid they'll never meet anyone else, they ignore the obvious signs of incompatibility. Others keep dating the wrong person because they feel guilty about breaking off a relationship. They're afraid of rejecting or hurting the other person. To avoid the guilt, sometimes people wait until things get so bad in the relationship that the other person has to break it off first.

To avoid making these common mistakes, it's important to listen to your intuition. Know yourself and trust yourself. Know that you deserve to be happy with the perfect person for you, and don't be willing to settle for less.

CHANGING PARTNERS

Sometimes, people keep dating the wrong person because they think they can help their partner change. They may like some of their date's qualities, but are unhappy with others, and think, with a little time and advice, they'll be able to fix the person.

On Eileen and Jeff's first date, Eileen could tell that Jeff had a drinking problem. In the two hours they spent together, Jeff drank four beers and two glasses of wine. Most of his conversation revolved around his favorite pastime—drinking.

Every bone in Eileen's body told her this was not the right person for her. But she wanted to be in a relationship so badly she decided to keep dating Jeff in hopes she could help him get sober. It wasn't until three months and many arguments later that Eileen realized Jeff didn't want to get sober. Eileen's intuition tried to tell her Jeff wasn't right for her, but she didn't pay attention to it.

On your first date, don't be afraid to ask a few questions about things that are important to you . A first date is a kind of fact-finding mission and while you don't want it to turn into an interrogation, it's okay to ask questions about your date's family, job, education, or anything else that will help you know if you are compatible. There's a difference between bombarding someone with a list of questions one right after the other, and naturally weaving your questions into the conversation. Use your "personal" and "ideal mate" inventories to guide you in getting to know your date better.

Just as you'll be sorting out who's right for you and who isn't, your date will be doing the same thing. That's why it's so important for you to be yourself on dates. The other person also has to gather information to decide whether to end the relationship after one date, proceed with caution, or go full steam ahead. Finding your perfect mate isn't about being critical, it's about finding a good match. So help your date do that by being yourself.

KNOWING WHEN IT'S RIGHT

As I mentioned in an earlier chapter, men and women fall in love with each other because of how they feel about themselves when they're together. You'll know you've found the perfect mate when you feel good about yourself when you're with that person.

After Holly's first date with Bernard, she felt better about herself than she had in years. When Holly described her work as a pediatric nurse, Bernard was filled with admiration. He told Holly how awed he was by her compassion and talent and the fact she must be making a tremendous difference in the lives of other people. Bernard saw qualities in Holly she had never even seen in herself. After their first date, Holly walked away feeling very good about herself and as if she might be falling in love with Bernard.

After Warren had his first date with Veronica, he had a whole new image of his body. Although he had been lifting weights during the past year, he knew he was destined to have a slight build with very little muscle definition. Veronica saw him differently and didn't hesitate to tell him so. She told him she thought he had a great build, and that because he had a smaller frame, his muscles stood out more. Warren wasn't sure exactly why, but he knew he wanted to go out with Veronica the next weekend.

Think about why you choose to spend time with some people but not with others. Chances are you surround yourself with people you feel good being with. Whether it's certain family members, co-workers, or friends, you gravitate toward people who build you up rather than tear you down.

I've always told the women in my classes that if you really like a man, give him the opportunity to feel good about himself by paying him a compliment. You can compliment him on his appearance, his sense of humor, his knowledge, his manners, or any other quality you admire. The same applies to a man. Don't assume a woman knows she dresses well or tells a funny story or is gracious. If you like something about your date, tell him or her! I'm convinced very attractive men and women rarely receive compliments, because everyone assumes they already know they're good looking. We all need to hear the good things about ourselves verbalized. Don't hold back a compliment, just because you assume the person is already aware of his or her good qualities.

THE NEXT DATE

At some point during your first date, you will begin to have a sense of whether or not you want to see this person again. In some cases, the suggestion for a next date will come at the end of your time together. In these cases, everything flowed. Conversation was easy, there was a physical attraction, and it was obvious neither of you wanted your date to end. In that case, seize the moment and ask for another date, suggesting a specific activity and time. Pick an activity you'd both enjoy, based on whatever mutual interests you have discovered on your first date.

Most of the time, however, it's best to give yourself a few days to reflect on your feelings about your date and the time you spent together. Remember, you're shopping around. Not only are you going to have to budget your dollars to accommodate lots of first dates, you're going to have to budget your time to allow yourself the opportunity to meet as many people as possible. There's no need to feel anxious or desperate. If you think this person is someone you want to see again, you can leave the door open to another date by saying you enjoyed yourself and would like to see him or her again soon. Suggest that you talk on the phone later in the week, and then call in a few days. If you're serious about another date, call and ask, even if your date seems hesitant.

Believe me, you'll get nothing in this world unless you ask for it, and that includes another date!

Sometimes, telling your date you will call will be the trigger that gives the other person enough confidence to come up with an idea for the next date.

Melody spent a great deal of her first date with Glen wondering if he would ask her out again. As they sat in the coffee shop of a local bookstore discussing their favorite authors, Melody thought Glen was having a good time, but she wasn't completely sure. She was afraid to suggest an activity for their next date until she got a clear signal from him that he wanted to see her again.

Finally, when it came time to say good-bye, Glen asked Melody if he could give her a call sometime. That was the signal Melody was looking for. She quickly invited Glen to a book fair that was taking place the following week. Glen accepted Melody's invitation on the spot.

If your instincts even hint that your date might want to see you again, then go for it. In the dating game, if you snooze, you lose. Getting turned down is not the worst thing that can happen. The worst thing that can happen is missing out on a second date with the perfect person for you because you didn't ask.

SAYING NO

There may be times when you'll want to see your date again, but won't like the activity the person suggests. There's a way to decline the activity without declining the invitation. For example, if your date asks you to go downhill skiing, and you hate the cold, tell your date you don't think you want to go skiing, but you wouldn't mind doing something else. When suggesting another activity, be specific. If you're vague, your date might think you're politely trying to get out of seeing him or her again.

After Melissa and Grant's afternoon date at an art gallery, Melissa asked Grant if he wanted to take a live model drawing class with her at the art institute. Although Grant loved looking at art, the only thing he had ever drawn were stick figures. The last thing he wanted to do was sit and struggle to draw a real human being. Instead of declining Melissa's invitation totally, he said that rather than take a drawing class, he would prefer to visit another art exhibit. Melissa was perfectly fine with his choice of activity, and they had a wonderful second date.

There may be times when you want to see your date again, but the day suggested is not a good one for you. In that case, you can say you'd love to get together again and suggest another time. When Marshal asked Anita for a second date for the following weekend, Anita said she was sorry but she would be out of town that weekend. She said she was free the weekend after that. Unfortunately, Marshal was traveling on that weekend. It took Anita and Marshal ten minutes to figure out another time to get together, but they didn't mind the time or effort it took. It was clear they wanted to see each other again and that's what mattered most.

There will probably be times when, after your first date, you will be asked for another date and you won't want to accept. If you are absolutely sure you don't want to see the person again, you must politely, but clearly, say no. If you aren't clear in saying no, you may end up leading the person on, and that would be unfair. Even though you may find it hard, don't avoid the issue or give the impression that you might accept an invitation at some future date by suggesting that the person call you later. It's possible to decline the invitation without rejecting the person. Always be friendly but firm. For example, you could tell the person that you enjoy his or her company, but aren't interested in a dating relationship.

There's no reason to feel guilty about not continuing to see someone who isn't right for you. People would much rather know up front that you're not interested in dating them, than find out a month later you never really wanted to continue dating. A first date is way too early in the dating game for anyone to feel rejected. You don't even really know each other yet. Turning down a second date isn't about rejection. It's about putting your energy into a serious search for your mate. Be honest and no one will get hurt.

Whether your first date turns into a second date or not, the important thing is that you *go* on your first date. Remember, a first date is an adventure. Unless you take that first step, you'll never know what's to follow.

CHAPTER 7: TAKE ACTION

A first date is a critical step in your search for the perfect mate. Don't let anxiety keep you from being clear-headed as you continue the interview process. Remember, you will be meeting lots of people. The better prepared you are for a first date, the better you will be able to analyze the results and avoid spending time with someone who isn't right for you.

1. Before beginning to make dates, prepare a list of possible meeting places, including names, addresses, phone numbers, and directions.

2. Make a list of possible activities you feel would be comfortable and appropriate for a first date for yourself and your prospective dates.

3. Select two or three outfits you know are flattering and comfortable to wear on a first date.

4. Find some foolproof way to be easily identified at your meeting place. It might be a brightly colored scarf, a distinctive hat, a flower, or a book.

5. If anxiety is a problem for you, before you go on a date practice breathing deeply and slowly. As you inhale, mentally recite "As I breath in, I feel calm." As you exhale, recite "As I breath out, I let go of tension."

6. Remember, opposites attract. In your journal, list some of your personality traits and the corresponding opposite traits. For example, if you are emotional and energetic, the opposite might be logical and calm; if you are spontaneous, the opposite might be cautious or methodical.

7. After your first date, take some time to analyze it. In your journal, list the positive qualities you saw in the person, as well as the negative qualities. Compare them to your "ideal mate" inventory.

8. As you analyze your date, think about things you might want to do differently on your next "first date." Did you ask enough questions? Were you authentic or did you pretend to be something you're not? Did you talk too much? Not enough? The purpose of this exercise is not to pick yourself apart, but to maximize your results. Be objective, not critical.

9. In your journal, write a paragraph or two about how you would like to feel when you are with your ideal mate.

Congratulations! You've come a long way on your journey to finding the perfect mate for you. You know your strengths and weaknesses and accept yourself. You know what you are looking for, and you're taking action to get what you want and deserve. Keep up the good work.

Dating with Children

YOU'RE MORE THAN JUST A PARENT

Some of you might be thinking, "I'd love to start dating, but who would want to date someone with four children, a dog, and two parakeets?" The answer is, plenty of people. Don't automatically assume just because you have children, you're less desirable. There are plenty of people who like children and who want to date someone with children. While other single parents are probably the most likely to be interested in dating someone with children, there are lots of people who have no children of their own who would be delighted with a ready-made family.

Even if you fit the description of single mom or dad, it's important for you to realize that you are more than just a parent. You are a vibrant, energetically alive adult who deserves to have a social life. To help make the transition from mommy or daddy to date, lover, boyfriend or girlfriend, stop thinking of yourself as just a parent, and start thinking of yourself as an attractive, devastatingly sexy single. To help boost your confidence, take more care with your appearance than you might be in the habit of doing. When you're out doing errands on the weekend, wear something that flatters you, even if it's just a pair of great-looking jeans, instead of wearing cutoffs or sweats.

Think about having a makeover. A different haircut and an updated wardrobe are both good ways to feel more attractive and desirable. If you're still wearing a wedding ring, take it off now. In fact, shed any rings that would convey the message that you're unavailable.

When Maria was ready to start dating again after her divorce, she looked in the mirror and didn't like what she saw. She decided to visit an image consultant, whose advice was very simple: Get rid of the long, outdated hairdo and the horn-rimmed glasses. Maria found a terrific hairdresser who gave her a hairstyle that was flattering and easy to care for. Then she went to the optometrist and was fitted for contact lenses. When Maria looked in the mirror after her makeover, instead of a rather dowdy mother-figure, she saw an attractive, young-looking woman who was ready to meet her perfect mate.

YOU CAN DO IT

Making the mental transition from parent to person is one thing, but there are also practical matters to be considered. Dating when you have children offers some challenges that aren't present when you are footloose and fancy free, but there is no reason why you can't be a parent and still have a rich and fulfilling social life. While you will need a bit more organization and some creativity to be a dating parent than if you were single without children, both you and your children will benefit from the extra effort.

I know how important it is to take care of your children; to meet their physical and emotional needs. But if you don't take care of yourself, you won't be able to take care of your children. Taking care of yourself first is what I call the "oxygen mask" principle. If you've ever taken a commercial airliner, you've heard the flight attendant tell passengers that if there should be a change in pressure and the oxygen mask drops down, parents should always breathe into it first before assisting their children. The theory is that if you don't get any oxygen, you'll be unable to help your child.

The same principle applies to your life in general. You have to take care of your own emotional, mental, and physical needs before you can help your children. If you're sacrificing your social life for your children, you're not doing them a favor. The best gift you can give your children is the example of a well-balanced, happy adult life. Everything you do and say and feel is a lesson for your children. When you take care of yourself emotionally by enjoying your life and the people who populate it, you're teaching your children how to become healthy, happy adults as well.

GUILTY AS CHARGED

As a parent, there are many times in life when you are faced with a conflict that may cause you to feel guilty. On the one hand, you have a desire to do something for yourself that would be pleasurable. On the other hand, you might feel guilty for:

- Spending the money

- Spending the time

- Any of the 101 other reasons parents can find to feel guilty

Suppose, for example, that you've been invited out on a date, but you aren't sure whether to accept or not. You feel guilty about leaving your small children with a baby-sitter or leaving your older children alone for a few hours. My advice is feel the guilt and do it anyway! If you don't, sooner or later you're going to resent the fact you never date or do anything socially. And who do you think your resentment's going to affect most? That's right. Your children. Believe me, your guilty feelings are much easier on your children than your feelings of anger and resentment.

When Miranda was invited to go on a date to see an ice show, her two school-age children whined and complained about being left with a baby-sitter. Miranda came very close to canceling her date, but realized she needed to get out and do something fun for a change. She hadn't been out in months and was beginning to feel resentful and cranky.

Although she felt the guilt that sometimes comes with being a parent, she went on her date anyway and managed to have a wonderful time. Her guilt didn't ruin her evening, but it did motivate her to buy each of her children a souvenir gift. Because she made the decision to go out in spite of feeling guilty, Miranda's children got a mom who was refreshed and energized—with the added bonus of a surprise gift. If Miranda had canceled her date, her children would have had their mother home with them, but she would have been irritable and angry—not a great role model for a happy parent.

NO PERMISSION NEEDED

I'm only going to say this once, so I want you to pay careful attention. You do not need approval from your children in order to date! Your decision to date must come from your own readiness to have a social life. When you feel ready and secure about your decision, your children will come to accept and eventually respect it. If you're undecided and look to them for permission to date, you may or may not get it, but one thing's for sure. You'll have given them control. You don't have to ask them if it's okay or if they'd mind if you go out. Just go, and have fun!

Audrey would never accept a date until she got permission from her thirteen-year-old daughter. She sincerely believed she was doing the right thing when she asked, "Honey, would you mind if I went out this weekend?" or "I'm going on a date tonight, okay sweetheart?" Audrey didn't realize, by asking permission, she was giving her daughter control of her social life. Her daughter took it willingly and used it freely to try to make her mother feel guilty. As a result, Audrey's daughter learned to be manipulative and lost respect for her mother.

To avoid conflict, some parents will keep their dating a secret from their children. But when you hide the fact that you're dating, you're still giving your children control. By dating secretly, you're telling your children that you're ashamed of what you're doing. Having a life outside of being a parent is nothing to be ashamed of. Your children need to know that while they are a very important part of your life, your entire world doesn't revolve around them. When you can be open with your children about your social life, it reduces their anxiety and builds trust. Explain to them that just as they need to have friends their own age, you need to have adult friendships. They'll soon catch on that they'll benefit from your happiness. If your children are getting the kind of love and attention they need from you, they won't be threatened by your dating.

Stephen had been divorced from his wife for two years when he met Linda at a dance for single parents. Stephen shared custody of his three children with their mother, who worked every night until 9 or 9:30. He was with the children every night of the week, as well as every other weekend. He also worked very long hours and moonlighted on weekends to earn extra money whenever he had the chance. This schedule left him very little time for dating. In fact, the night he met Linda was the first time he had been out socially in the two years he had been single. They hit it off and started seeing each as often as time would allow, but Stephen never told his children he was dating. Of course, it didn't take long for his thirteen-year-old daughter to know something was going on. Suddenly her father wasn't always available, as he had been before. She overheard comments from other members of the family. One Sunday morning, on the kitchen sink she found an earring she knew didn't belong to her.

Christy kept waiting for her father to sit down and talk to her about his new girlfriend. When he didn't, Christy was hurt. Her father's dating wasn't the problem. The problem was his silence. Finally, Christy approached an aunt, who gave her some very good advice. She told Christy that when parents have children, they don't come with an instruction manual; that her dad probably really wanted to talk to Christy, but wasn't sure how. She told Christy she could help her father by bringing up the subject herself. Christy did, and everyone was relieved to finally have the truth out in the open, but a lot of pain and anguish could have been avoided if Stephen had just been honest in the first place.

A PACKAGE DEAL

Not only must you be honest with your children, you must also be honest with the people you are dating. Whatever you do, don't ever hide the fact you have children. Be clear that you are a package deal and proud of it! Hiding the fact you have children or postponing telling your date the truth is not the way to begin a healthy relationship.

Andrew and Tracy had three dates before he learned she had children. Tracy had every intention of telling Andrew about her three young children on their first date, but it seemed as if it weren't the right time. It was the same on their next date. She knew she had to tell him, but she was so afraid Andrew wouldn't want to be involved with her once he found out she was a parent that she kept avoiding it.

On their third date, Tracy reached into her coat pocket for a tissue and a pacifier fell to the floor. When Andrew picked it up, he asked Tracy why she was carrying around a pacifier. Finally, Tracy told Andrew the truth. Although he was stunned, Andrew was also very excited. Fortunately for Tracy, Andrew loved children and told Tracy he was really looking forward to meeting hers. If she had told the truth from the beginning, Tracy would have been spared the stress of concealing that she had children. But more importantly, what was the point of lying in the first place? If he didn't want to date someone with children, why would Tracy want Andrew?

NEW BEGINNINGS

Beginning to date again can be an exciting new chapter in your life, but finding time to meet a new mate, when you can barely find time to do the dishes, can be a challenge. Don't let lack of time keep you from the happiness you deserve. While there are many ways to meet a potential mate, the personal ads and the Internet are tailor-made for you. You can put together your personal ad and have a wonderful time talking to your potential new dates while your children are asleep or busy with their own activities. In addition, if you have a computer, you can visit the Web sites on the Internet that are devoted to dating without leaving the comfort of your home.

As you prepare to place a personal ad, review the information in chapter 3 and note, in particular, my advice that you be specific. When you're placing your ad, the fact you're a single parent must be included. Remember, the beauty of a personal ad is that it helps you target exactly the kind of person you want to meet. If you have children, you want to meet someone who's comfortable dating someone with children, so don't hesitate to advertise that you are a single parent.

Sylvia had two children, a seven-year-old and a ten-year-old. She'd been a single mother for four years, and she was ready for a relationship. But between working, volunteering in her children's classrooms, and shuffling them to their various activities, she didn't have time to spend trying to meet a man.

Placing a personal ad was perfect for her. She could write it at home and listen to her voice mail messages after her children were in bed. Sylvia's ad read as follows:

> Divorced, energetic single mom, 29, with full custody and loving it, desires someone who loves kids.

Sylvia could have said more about herself, but she wanted to make sure readers knew she was a devoted single mother. On her voice mail she went into more detail about herself.

> Hi! Thanks for calling. You've reached a very happy single mom who loves living with her two adorable children, ages seven and ten. I'm busy with my kids, but I have lots of other interests, including rollerblading, hiking, and watching old movies. If you'd like to spend time with me and get to know my great kids, please leave a message. Thanks again for calling!

Sylvia's voice mail showed that she had a life separate from her children, but she was still very clear that her children were a priority.

Either in your ad or on your voice mail message, mention the ages of your children. While your children's ages won't matter to many people, some people have definite preferences. Some like teenagers, but are uncomfortable with younger children. Others enjoy little children, but don't know how to relate to teens. You want your future dates to be completely comfortable around your children, so it's only fair to tell them up front how old your children are.

In addition to using a personal ad or the Internet to meet people, there are many groups dedicated specifically to single parents. While meeting other single parents is more likely if you go places with your children, don't limit yourself to these activities. Get out and do something just for yourself. Take a class where you'll meet members of the opposite sex or look for a special interest group for singles such as a hiking, biking, or theater group. Take up folk dancing or country-western dancing (it's good exercise and you don't need a partner).

CHILDREN CAN BE THE BRIDGE

Meeting people when you're with your children is often easier than when you're alone. Children make you more approachable. Someone who might not know how to start a conversation with you, might feel very comfortable talking to your child.

For example, Mary Jo's son, Billy, was the excuse Stanley used to meet Mary Jo. Stanley was in line behind Mary Jo and Billy as they waited in line to get on the ski lift. Stanley commented on Billy's skis and asked how he liked them. In no time, the three of them were swapping ski stories and riding up the hill on the same chair. They ended up spending the entire afternoon together and at the end of the day Stanley asked Mary Jo for her phone number. They've been dating now for several months.

A child also brought Corrine and Marcus together. Well, actually two children. When she was shopping for a birthday present for her nephew in the boy's section of a department store, Corrine noticed a nice-looking man with twin boys who looked about the same age as her nephew. Corrine wasn't sure what style jeans were popular with an eleven-year-old, so she walked up to one of the twins and asked him.

As Corrine and his son talked about the latest in boys' fashions, Marcus came over and introduced himself. While his boys tried on clothes, Marcus and Corrine continued talking. By the time the boys had decided on their purchases, Corrine and Marcus had a date for dinner.

Corrine and Marcus's meeting was obviously not planned. Whether you want to call it destiny or just a coincidence, they probably would never have met if Marcus hadn't gone shopping with his children.

Being a single parent gives you some great opportunities to meet other single parents. Your own children are your best resource for places to go where you might meet other single parents. If your children like going somewhere, so will other children. Along with other children, come other parents— many of whom are single. The following are just a few of the places you can expect to meet other single parents: zoos, carnivals, children's museums, playgrounds, libraries, and video arcades, and that's just the tip of the iceberg. I suggest you sit down with a friend who's a single parent and brainstorm all the places you can think of where parents take children.

Manny met his future wife at his son's Little League game. Every Saturday morning, Manny and his son Matt would show up at the ballpark at 9 o'clock sharp. One Saturday, Manny found himself sitting next to a very attractive woman whose son was playing on the opposite team. They talked about their sons, where they went to school, what grade they were in, and when Manny managed to see Diane wasn't wearing a wedding ring, he asked about her son's father. He learned she was a widow, and she learned he was divorced. The next Saturday, his son's game was earlier than her son's, but Manny and his son stayed around to watch, and he and Diane got to know each other a little better. They decided to take the boys out for pizza after the game and became a blended family before the next baseball season started.

Pamela lived very close to a water park, which she and her children visited frequently during the summer. While her children had fun on the water slides, Pamela would sit in a lounge chair and observe the other parents and children. It was while people-watching that Pamela first noticed Eric. She had seen him several times during the summer and always enjoyed watching him play with his children. Unlike a lot of the other parents, Eric joined his children on the water slides and laughed happily as his children jumped on him, splashed him, and chased him.

Finally, one Saturday afternoon Pamela decided to introduce herself to him. When Eric went to the snack bar, Pamela hurried to stand in line behind him. She knew he always ordered a lot of food for his children, so she offered to help him carry it to his table. As they chatted about the high price of hot dogs and pizza, Eric asked Pamela if she and her children wanted to join his family at their table. Their children spent the rest of the day going down water slides together while Eric and Pamela got to know each other. Now that they're married, a water park is always included in their family vacations.

MATCHMAKER, MATCHMAKER, MAKE ME A MATCH

Another way for you to meet new people is to let your children do the matchmaking. I've known lots of men and women whose children have introduced them to the person who ended up being their mate. If your children approve of the person enough to introduce him or her to you, it's definitely worth a try.

Seventeen-year-old Clayton played quarterback for his high school football team. His mother, Sandra, came to every one of his games. Clayton had always thought his football coach and his mother would make a good couple, but he never said anything to either one of them. Finally, after the last game of the season, Clayton dragged his mother over to meet his coach and invited him to dinner for the next night. Sandra was shocked and embarrassed at her son's boldness, but she went along with it. She prepared her special lasagna and Clayton's coach stayed late into the night, talking. That was twelve years ago, and Clayton's mother has never stopped thanking her son for introducing her to the man who became her husband.

In a similar way, Samantha played cupid for her father. Samantha had been a Girl Scout for two years, and during that time she had always had the same leader. When she heard they were to get a new leader, Samantha wasn't sure whether she'd like her or not. As it turned out, she liked her new leader so much that she decided to figure out a way for her dad and her leader to meet. When it came time to sell Girl Scout cookies, Samantha enlisted her father to be the cookie dad, knowing that he'd have to talk a lot with the leader about the cookie drive. She just knew if they spent time talking, they would really like each other. She was right. By the time the cookie drive was over, Samantha's dad and her Girl Scout leader were dating and by the time next year's cookie drive came around, Samantha's Girl Scout leader was also her stepmother.

INTRODUCING YOUR DATES TO YOUR CHILDREN

Although I recommend dating a lot of people in order to find the perfect match for you, I don't recommend introducing all your dates to your children. When you have children, an open-door policy when it comes to dating is not a good idea. Meeting every, or even most, of those you go out with can only upset and confuse them. Children are always most comfortable when their world is predictable, and a steady diet of new dates will keep them constantly off-balance. Until someone comes into your life who you feel is special and has become important to you, be very selective about whom you introduce your children to.

How much time should pass before you introduce the new person in your life to your children? Unfortunately, there is no right answer to that question. The time-frame will be different for everyone, depending on the individual and the circumstances. You may know within the first four or five dates that this person is special and is in your life to stay. Or, it may take months before you feel confident that you are committed to each other.

Keep in mind that once they have met, your children will undoubtedly begin to bond with your new partner, maybe even develop a strong affection for them. Then, if the relationship comes to an untimely end, your children will suffer a sense of loss. By waiting to introduce your children to your partner until you feel quite sure of the relationship, you can avoid exposing your children to possible hurt. Until that time comes, there are lots of ways to spend time together without your children being involved.

Whatever you do, don't try to side-step the inconvenience of meeting outside of your home by having your date come over after the children are in bed. There are too many opportunities for disaster. The last thing you want is for your child to wake up and find you entertaining a stranger in the living room. It's not that you're doing something wrong—you're not! It's just best to avoid subjecting your child to some pretty strong feelings of shock and betrayal.

Sonya and Dick had been dating for seven weeks, but Sonya had not yet introduced Dick to her children. They were still in the "getting acquainted" stage, and she didn't want to rush things with her children. One night, Sonya's baby-sitter had to leave much earlier than usual, so after they had been out to dinner, Sonya decided to invite Dick back to her house. It was late in the evening, long after her children's bedtime, and she was sure her children would be sound asleep. After the baby-sitter went home, Sonya and Dick talked over a cup of coffee. Unfortunately, Sonya's eight-year-old daughter woke up and was shocked and frightened to find her mother in the living room with a strange man. Dick felt so awkward that he left immediately and Sonya had the unpleasant task of explaining the situation to her children and trying to rebuild the trust that had been broken.

WHEN THE TIME IS RIGHT

While it's best to wait to introduce your children to someone until you're sure they are special, it's all right to mention them by name, saying "I'm going out to dinner tonight with so and so," when you start seeing them on a regular basis. When it's time to introduce them, tell your children that this is someone you like very much and introduce the person as a good friend, rather than as your boyfriend or girlfriend.

Be prepared for your children to be unfriendly to your new friend at first. Although you see this person as having only wonderful qualities, your children may see him or her as a threat. It's easy to understand how they might object to sharing you with another person.

While it's important for your children to show respect and courtesy toward you and your date, it's even more important for you to listen to and understand their feelings. Keep the lines of communication with your children open, so they can ask questions or talk about their fears. Reassure your children that your love for them will never change, no matter who you date. Also reassure them that no one will ever replace their other parent and never, ever tell your children you are looking for a new mother or father for them. If you are divorced, they already have a mother or a father and they may wonder what will become of them. If you are widowed, your children's memory of their mother or father should always be respected and cherished for the special relationship it is.

FIRST ENCOUNTERS

The first time your children and your new partner spend time together, it should be in neutral territory, not in your (the children's) home. Your first impulse may be to invite your new love for a nice, cozy family dinner at your house, but this is not a good idea. It is also your children's house, and they may feel their territory is being invaded.

For their first time together, select an activity that your children enjoy. Roller skating, going to the beach or a playground, or visiting the zoo are a few ideas that might work for you. Whatever you decide to do, avoid strictly adult activities such as going to the symphony or dining at a formal restaurant.

The first time Brian's children spent time with Jill, they went to a very elegant restaurant. Not only were Brian's son and daughter less than thrilled to meet his new friend, they were unhappy about having to get dressed up. Brian's twelve-year-old son spent most of the evening complaining that he couldn't breathe because his tie was too tight, and his fourteen-year-old daughter, who lived in jeans, was angry that she had to wear a dress for "some dumb lady." It was a bad plan, but fortunately, Brian and Jill had a sense of humor and were able to laugh about their mistake. By the end of the evening, the children were laughing too, and now it's one of those "remember when" stories that never fails to get a good giggle from everyone.

To improve the chances your children will react well to your new love, be sure they're as comfortable as possible in their surroundings. If their first experience together is a negative experience, it'll be harder to turn it into a positive experience the next time.

Linda's children loved going to the amusement park, so she planned for her new love interest, Dave, to go along with them one Sunday. It was a very successful day. Linda's children weren't forced to spend long periods of time alone with Dave, but could have short conversations with him between roller coaster rides instead. By the end of the day, each of Linda's children had ridden a roller coaster with Dave and had gotten to see the fun, childlike side of him. Linda was smart to make sure her children were comfortable and having fun when they first spent time with Dave. When they said good-bye late that evening, they had a positive impression of him—one that they could build upon.

OVERCOMING OBSTACLES

It doesn't matter if your children are toddlers, teenagers, or adults, having a social life forces you to consider issues you'd never think about if you were dating without children. Whether it's baby-sitters, providing adequate supervision for older children, or upsetting your adult children's sensibilities, the challenges are there and must be dealt with.

If you have young children, your social life depends a lot on the availability of child care. Without someone to baby-sit, you can't go anywhere. Take an inventory of the people in your life who can provide this valuable service. Grandparents, teachers, older students who can be trusted, friends, neighbors, and baby-sitting services are all possible resources. Many people find that their best opportunity for dating comes during the times when the children are with their other parent. No matter whom you choose, don't put all your eggs in one basket.

Sheri's neighbor Thelma, a woman in her sixties who loved children and was very reliable, had watched Sheri's four- and six-year-old girls since they were born. There had never been a need for Sheri to have a back-up baby-sitter, because Thelma was always available and the girls loved her. When it became necessary for Thelma to be in the hospital for surgery, Sheri's social life changed drastically. Sheri's children had never been exposed to anyone but Thelma, and it was very hard for them to adjust to someone new. Sheri tried many baby-sitters before she found someone who was an acceptable replacement for the beloved Thelma. When she finally found someone both she and the children felt good about, she determined not to make the same mistake she had made in the past. When Thelma was able to sit again, Sheri used her, of course, but she also continued to use the new sitter so that she would never be left without a sitter again.

It's very important to have several baby-sitters you trust and know your children feel comfortable with. That way, if you accept a date with someone, and your baby-sitter cancels, you'll have another one in the wings who can take over at a moment's notice.

Another factor to consider when you're dating with young children, is how long you can stay out. Before you had children, you could stay out as late as you wanted to. You could party all night and sleep all day, and the only person who would suffer would be you. Not any more. First of all, your baby-sitter probably has to be home by a certain time, but more importantly, you need your energy to be a good parent the next day.

While you may not be able to burn the midnight oil as you could in the past, it's still possible to have a wonderful time with your date and be fresh for your children the next day. It just takes a little planning and creativity. Whenever possible, do something together during the daytime or in the early evening. Meet right after work for an early dinner or movie. If you go to the theater, skip the after-theater supper or drinks. If you go dancing, go early and leave after the second set. While it may not be fashionable to arrive at the club right when the music starts, there are advantages. The floor is less crowded, it's easier to find a table, and the service is better. Even though you can't stay out late as you did before you had children, you can still have a fun and exciting date.

Dating when you have teenage children is much different than dating with young children. While they may not need a baby-sitter, they still need supervision, even if it's yours, applied in advance. Before you go out on a date, you and your teenager need to discuss his or her plans for the time you'll be gone. Will your teen be home, or at a friend's? Will the friend's parents be home? Will your teenager be going out on a date of his or her own? If your teen is going out, where will he or she be and when will he or she be home?

If you don't have one already, carrying a pager provides a tremendous feeling of comfort when you have children of any age. Knowing you can be reached no matter where you are gives you the freedom to enjoy whatever it is you're doing without worry or stress. If your children know they will be late coming home or if they should need you for any reason, they will be able to contact you easily.

Although dating when you have adult children is less complicated than dating with teenagers or young children, there still may be some issues you'll have to deal with. If you have lost a spouse, your adult children may have difficulty adjusting to the idea of you dating or becoming involved in a relationship. Although they may not be as outspoken as a young child might be, adult children can be just as hurt or resentful about a new step-parent as a five-year-old.

Vince started dating Laura a year and a half after his wife passed away. He missed his wife very much, but was very lonely and didn't want to spend the rest of his life alone. When his daughter learned that he was dating someone, she was very upset. Vince talked to his daughter and listened to her feelings, but continued dating Laura because he knew it was the right thing for him to do.

It took a long time, but eventually Vince's daughter came to see that while Laura was different from her mother, she was good for her father. With Laura in his life, Vince started to live again. He and Laura joined a gym, took long walks on the beach every day, and Vince changed from a bitter, unhappy old man to a vigorous, youthful seventy-nine-year-old.

No matter how old they are, your children will have feelings about you dating, but you can't let them control your life. Let me remind you that you are responsible for your own happiness. You must not allow anyone, not even your children, to prevent you from having the happiness you deserve.

CHAPTER 8: TAKE ACTION

While dating with children presents some challenges, learning to balance your responsibilities with fun is well worth the effort. The exercises below will help you develop a plan that will allow you to be a parent who dates, but one who does so wisely.

1. Before you can take care of your children's needs, you have to take care of yourself. In your journal, make a list of all the things you can do to take care of your physical and emotional needs. Your list could include such things as: taking a bubble bath, playing a game of golf, or spending an afternoon with a good friend.

2. Sometimes parents let guilt keep them from taking care of themselves. In your journal, list three things you've always wanted to do, but haven't because you would feel guilty. Then describe how you'd feel if you went ahead and did what you wanted to do and how your children would benefit.

3. The Internet and the personal ads are convenient ways to meet people when your life is very busy. Put together a personal ad and voice mail message that portray you as a sexy single, as well as a single parent.

4. The best places to meet single parents are places you'd take your children. In your journal, list as many of these places as you can think of.

5. Until you feel sure that the person you are dating is someone special, it's not a good idea to introduce them to your children. In your journal, list all the ways you can think

of to meet your date without having them come to your home or having your children meet them.

6. When you do decide your children and your new love interest should meet, it needs to be on neutral ground and somewhere your children will feel comfortable. In your journal, make a list of appropriate places to take your children on their first encounter with your new partner.

Remember, for your children to be happy, you have to be happy. Finding your perfect mate is a goal you can be proud of—one that will benefit both you and your children. So pick yourself up, dust yourself off, and start all over again.

Are You Ready for a Commitment?

YOU'VE FOUND THE RIGHT PERSON

Congratulations! Your actions have paid off. You've found someone you really like and he or she likes you. You've been seeing each other for a while and are getting along well. (Everything adds up.) There's chemistry between the two of you, your mate meets your expectations for your ideal partner, and your values and goals are compatible. You're sure you've got a match. Does that mean you're ready for a commitment?

It might. Or, it might not.

JUST YOU AND ME

The first sign of commitment in a relationship is usually when both partners decide they want to see each other exclusively.

You may have been dating other people as well as each other, but now you have decided that your feelings for one another are strong enough that you don't want to share your time with anyone else.

Before you agree to date each other exclusively, you need to discuss your feelings about not dating other people openly with each other. If you have been open and honest with each other up to this point, this discussion will be easy and just a natural extension of the trust you are building in your relationship as you become closer. Dating exclusively is a decision both of you must be willing to make. If one of you were to agree to date exclusively before you were ready, it could lead to a breach of trust that would be difficult to repair.

Norm and Joy began dating after meeting at a mutual friend's Christmas party. For the first six weeks, they continued to date other people as well as each other. One evening, Norm told Joy that whenever he was on a date with another person, all he could think about was her. He asked if they could take their relationship to the next level and see each other exclusively.

Joy really liked Norm and didn't want to lose him so, instead of telling him there was another man in her life she liked equally well, she agreed to an exclusive relationship. Obviously, Norm was ready for a level of commitment that Joy was not. Without telling Norm about it, Joy continued to see the other man occasionally. Eventually, Norm began to sense that Joy's feelings for him were not as strong as his were toward her. When he mustered up the courage to confront her, Joy confessed she was seeing someone else and wasn't ready for an exclusive commitment. Joy's deception hurt Norm and destroyed any trust he had felt in her. He ended their relationship.

The main reason Joy and Norm's relationship ended was because they didn't have enough honesty in their relationship to discuss their feelings openly. Joy should never have agreed to see Norm exclusively when she wasn't ready for a committed relationship. If she had been honest, Norm could have put his desire for a commitment on hold and perhaps, in time, Joy would have come to want an exclusive relationship with Norm as much as he wanted one with her. By failing to be honest, she destroyed any chance for the relationship to survive and grow.

Before you make a commitment to an exclusive relationship, it's important that you understand what you're agreeing to. If you're not ready to see this person to the exclusion of all others, do not promise to do so. If you're not ready, or really not that interested, it's perfectly okay. But you must be honest with both yourself and your partner. If you allow yourself to become involved in an exclusive relationship when you aren't committed to the idea, you are cheating both yourself and the other person. If you cut yourself off from dating other people before you're ready for that level of commitment, you'll eventually come to feel you've settled for less than what you wanted, or you'll cheat on the other person, compromising your integrity as well as the relationship.

BEING IN SYNC

When one of you feels stronger about your relationship than the other, it's pretty obvious. Neither one of you is completely comfortable. The partner who feels the strongest is hurt by the other's distance. By the same token, the partner who feels less committed may experience some feelings of guilt.

If your feelings and your partner's aren't in sync, don't lose hope. Being on different rungs of the ladder doesn't mean your relationship is doomed for failure. Your partner may just need a little more time before joining you on the next step. Don't rush things. Be patient, and allow your partner to adjust to the next phase of commitment at his or her own pace.

Abby and Joel had been dating for eight months and Abby knew she wanted to be with Joel for the rest of her life. She had never felt as warm, secure, and cared for as she did when she was with Joel. Christmas was coming soon and Abby secretly hoped that Joel would surprise her with an engagement ring.

Joel cared very much for Abby, but he wasn't ready to ask Abby to marry him. For Christmas, he gave her a gold bracelet, not the engagement ring she had hoped for. When Abby opened her present and saw the bracelet instead of a ring, she hid her disappointment. She knew she and Joel were right for each other, so she decided to put her desire to be engaged on the back burner and wait until Joel was as ready as she was to make a commitment. Within six months, Joel felt the same way about Abby as she did about him and she got the engagement ring she wanted so badly.

While patience is a virtue and is often necessary in the course of a relationship, is there a limit to how long you should wait for your partner to step up to the plate? You certainly don't want to end your relationship prematurely, but you don't want to spend the rest of your life waiting for your mate to make a commitment either.

I'll never forget this story, told to me by a woman I met at one of my lectures.

"Saul and I had been dating off and on since our mid-thirties. After thirteen years, we finally decided to date each other exclusively. As soon as we committed to an exclusive relationship, Saul wanted to whisk me off to a nearby chapel and get married, but I wasn't ready. I wanted to date exclusively for a while before taking the next step.

"Saul was very patient, but every year he repeated his desire to get married. I continued to hesitate, and Saul, bless his heart, was willing to wait for as long as it would take. Unfortunately, it took too long. Four years after he first proposed marriage, Saul died of a heart attack. How I wish I could turn back the clock. I knew he was the one I wanted to spend my life with, but I thought I had forever to make that commitment."

Besides the obvious feelings of affection and desire, there are two things to look for when deciding whether your relationship has a future worth waiting for. First, are you both able to communicate openly about your feelings for each other, and second, is your partner making a genuine effort to create a close relationship with you? When those two things occur, a commitment will be the natural outcome.

FALLING IN LOVE WITH LOVE

I want to caution you here about the danger of falling in love with love. If, after a few dates with someone, you're daydreaming about the wedding ceremony, a honeymoon on a tropical isle, and a house in the suburbs with a white picket fence, you're probably in need of a reality check. While you may be having some very powerful feelings of love, it's too soon to make a mature commitment. You're just getting to know each other.

After seven dates with Jacqueline, Vincent was sure he wanted to spend the rest of his life with her. He couldn't stop thinking about her and their future together. He pictured them on their honeymoon, signing the lease for their first apartment, and planning their first family vacation. Vincent was so infatuated with Jacqueline and their new relationship, that he pretty much skipped the stage of their relationship where they got to know each other and shared their goals, dreams, and values. He jumped right to the commitment stage, without really knowing the woman he wanted to commit the rest of his life to.

One of the things Vincent didn't understand was that Jacqueline was a serious career woman. She was an executive with a large corporation and her job came first. Vincent was so busy fantasizing about their future and the vacations they would take together, that he failed to discover the most basic facts. One of them was that Jacqueline would never consider taking time off from her job to go anywhere.

Before you commit to each other, you must learn as much about each other as possible. As you share your feelings, fears, dreams, and goals, you must be honest and truthful. Commitment and trust go hand-in-hand. In a committed relationship, honesty and authenticity are imperative. If one of you holds back important information, your relationship is in grave danger.

Louise and Mel dated for just a few weeks before they committed to an exclusive relationship, but they spent almost a year learning about each other before they got married. From time to time during their courtship, Mel would talk about his dreams of having a family someday. Louise always listened attentively, but didn't say much, and Mel naturally assumed Louise felt the same way he did about having children. In reality, the idea of being a parent frightened Louise. She wasn't sure she had the patience to have children and it seemed like an awesome responsibility.

It wasn't until Mel and Louise had been married for more than a year and Mel suggested starting a family that Louise revealed her true feelings about having children. Mel was stunned. He had always believed Louise wanted children as much as he did. For the next several months, Mel struggled to understand how Louise could have married him without telling him the truth about her reluctance to have children.

Their relationship didn't survive.

Later, Louise admitted that she was afraid if she had told Mel she didn't want children, he would have broken off their engagement.

She's right, he probably would have. On the other hand, if Louise had been honest with Mel, there's always the possibility that he might have decided he could live without having children. It is always easier to handle the truth, however unpleasant, than it is to deal with manipulation and deception.

By now you should be getting the message. If you can't tell each other the truth, you can't have a committed relationship. When honesty is at the core of your relationship, you'll always feel safe and secure with each other.

Deanna had told Bobby almost everything about herself. He knew about her most embarrassing moments, about the classes she flunked in college, and about the time she got fired from a job. But, there was one thing she hadn't told him. Deanna had suffered an emotional breakdown a few years before she met Bobby. She hadn't told him because she was afraid he would think she was crazy.

Finally, she found the courage to tell him about her illness and the two weeks she spent in a psychiatric hospital. When Bobby heard Deanna's story, he was very loving and support-ive. He asked lots of questions so he could understand as much as possible about her ordeal and told her how brave she was to get the help she needed. The part of her past that Deanna thought of as a weakness turned out to be something Bobby admired her for.

IF YOU REALLY CARE

Real commitment is unconditional. That means loving your mate even when they're unlovable. It's easy to love someone who's considerate, accommodating, and generally nice to you. But what about those times when your mate is irritable, frustrated, or in a rotten mood? Although the last thing you feel like doing is loving them, that's exactly what they need the most.

If you're ready for a commitment, this won't be as hard as it sounds. On the other hand, if the idea of loving your mate even when they're unlovable sounds like something you couldn't possibly do, then you're not ready for a commitment.

Latisha and Lionel had dated for eight months. With each passing day, Latisha was more and more convinced that Lionel was the "one." They had the same interests, the same goals and dreams. They laughed easily together, and when they danced together they looked like pros. Latisha couldn't imagine being with anyone else.

One evening, when Lionel picked Latisha up for a dinner date, he wasn't his usual upbeat self. He seemed down and depressed and Latisha was annoyed by his behavior. Instead of being concerned, she became indignant. Latisha took Lionel's bad mood personally and blamed him for ruining their evening. When he took her home, she stormed into the house without kissing him goodnight.

The next day, when Lionel called to apologize for his bad mood the night before, Latisha shocked him by telling him their relationship was over. Lionel tried to explain that his mood had nothing to do with her, but Latisha didn't care. She said she didn't want to put up with a moody person.

Obviously, Latisha wasn't ready for a commitment. In a committed relationship, you will love your partner when they are down, as well as when they are up.

YOU CAN HAVE IT ALL

Sometimes people make a commitment to each other, not because they are sure this is the right person, but because they think they should. Think twice before making a commitment for any of the following reasons:

- Everybody else in your group of friends is married

- You're feeling pressure from your family

- You're worried about your biological clock running out

- You are afraid to face the future alone

- You are seeking financial security

- It's easier to get married than to break up

While some of the above reasons for making a commitment may seem compelling, if the person isn't the right one for you, you will probably come to regret your decision. Don't settle. Choose your lifetime partner with the belief that you can have it all—romance, passion, friendship, and lasting love. If you intuitively feel that this person's not right for you, you need to move on.

Annie and Terry had dated each other exclusively for several months. Annie enjoyed her time with Terry, but with every date came the strong feeling that he wasn't the person she wanted to spend the rest of her life with. Annie knew that Terry wanted to marry her someday, so she decided the best thing for both of them would be to end the relationship as soon as possible. Annie understood that Terry would be very hurt and disappointed, but knew that his pain would be far greater if she were to keep dating him in spite of her misgivings.

Some people are afraid to make a long-term commitment even though they know they've found the person they want to spend the rest of their life with. When that happens, it's wise to gain as much knowledge as possible about relationships. Once you know how to keep passion, communication, romance, and intimacy alive in your relationship, confidence replaces fear.

Gavin had dated Mary Beth for two years and he loved her very much, but whenever Mary Beth wanted to talk about their future together, Gavin avoided the topic. Gavin had been married before, and it had been a very traumatic relationship.

Whenever Mary Beth said the "M" word, Gavin's stomach knotted up and he broke into a cold sweat. As much as he loved Mary Beth, he was fearful that he wasn't marriage material. He'd failed at one relationship, what if he failed again?

Mary Beth understood Gavin's doubts, so she invited him to attend one of my lectures with her. She knew that she and Gavin could have a lasting relationship. All he needed was the confidence that he could learn the skills needed to nurture and sustain a marriage. Attending my lecture was Gavin's first step toward a lifetime commitment to Mary Beth—a commitment to learn about and practice the behaviors that would keep their feelings for each other alive forever.

FOR IT TO WORK, YOU HAVE TO WORK

To live "happily ever after" with your chosen mate requires a commitment to do whatever it takes to keep that lovin' feelin'. Maintaining a successful relationship is very similar to maintaining a successful career. Seminars, journal articles, professional courses, team-building workshops, training in communication skills, lectures, books, motivational tapes— they're all important to a successful career. Your personal life deserves and demands the same kind of diligence.

To reap the benefits of a healthy loving relationship, you must continually strive to enhance your relationship skills. You must read books and magazines, go to lectures, take workshops and seminars, listen to tape programs, and even seek counseling if necessary, to improve your relationship. New information leads to new behavior. As long as you continue to get new information, you'll continue to improve the way you relate to each other.

Warren and Eve had been dating for six months. They were so happy planning their future together that they never dreamed their relationship might need help. It wasn't until Eve lost her job that they discovered they handled stress differently. Eve needed to talk things through when she was confused or angry. When Warren was upset, he shut down. Warren couldn't understand how Eve could go on and on about her job loss, and Eve was very disappointed by Warren's insensitivity.

Thinking that she and Warren would never be able to resolve this difference in communication styles, Eve had decided to end their relationship when she saw my infomercial. She ordered my program, *Light His Fire* and asked Warren to listen to the program for men, *Light Her Fire*.

Warren came to understand that his behavior stemmed from his childhood. He had been raised in a household where feelings were not talked about. In his home, silence was praised as the proper way to handle feelings. As Warren gained an understanding about his behavior, he began to understand that he and Eve were different. He realized he needed to allow Eve to talk about her feelings when she was stressed and he needed to share his feelings with her as well. Because Eve and Warren were willing to get help, a serious misunderstanding was resolved and their relationship was saved.

AN OUNCE OF PREVENTION

I know this isn't a very romantic analogy, but your relationship is a lot like a car. You know if you don't do preventive maintenance on your car, it will eventually break down and possibly die. You have to keep it fueled up, rotate the tires, change the oil, and take it in for regular tune-ups to keep it running smoothly.

You have to do the same thing for your relationship. Just as you wouldn't let your car run out of gas or your tires wear down to nothing, don't wait until your relationship is in trouble to take care of it. By doing things on a regular basis to strengthen your relationship, you can avoid the possibility of the pain and heartache that so often come when a relationship has been neglected.

When we plant a new garden, we give it lots of loving care: we water it every day, pull the weeds as soon as they appear, and fertilize it regularly to keep it thriving. A new relationship is nurtured in much the same way. You kiss each other hello and good-bye, you touch each other a lot, you call each other every day, you're considerate of each other and eager to listen to each other's opinions and feelings, you buy each other little gifts and remember food preferences.

We've all seen gardens that have suffered years of neglect. The novelty has worn off and the garden has died from lack of water and it is overgrown with weeds. The same thing can happen in a relationship. Once a couple is secure in their commitment, they begin to take each other for granted.

One of you might say you'll call the other and then don't. You may forget to hug and kiss the way you used to. A passionate kiss at the end of the day becomes a quick peck on the lips. In my recent book, *The 10-Second Kiss*, I tell readers they have to do three times as much to keep their mate as they did to get their mate. That means giving them a 5-second compliment, a 10-second kiss, and a 20-second hug every day.

Your commitment to each other means you are willing to work at being each other's number one priority. Whether that means calling every day to say "I love you," planning surprise dates, or leaving love notes for each other, you have to work at keeping the romantic spark alive in your relationship.

When Wendy and Patrick first became involved, they were extremely considerate and thoughtful of each other. When she went grocery shopping Wendy always picked up a pound of Patrick's favorite coffee. Patrick called Wendy every day to tell her he loved her. They both planned surprise dates for each other. Wendy still remembers the time Patrick came to her door carrying a blindfold. Placing it over her eyes, he led her to his car and drove her to a nearby lake where he had earlier placed a table and chairs, laid out with an elegant picnic supper for two.

About two years into their relationship, they began taking each other for granted. Wendy became so preoccupied with her job that she neglected to pick up Patrick's favorite coffee at the grocery store. Patrick's daily phone calls dwindled to once a week instead of once a day, and it had been months since either of them had surprised the other with anything. Their relationship was quickly losing its sizzle.

Fortunately, they received *The 10-Second Kiss* as a gift just when they needed it most. They read it together and realized that the way to get the fun and excitement back in their relationship was to remember what they had done in the beginning of their relationship, and treat each other the way they had then.

LOVE MEANS BEING ABLE TO SAY YOU'RE SORRY

There are two very important skills that are necessary for any committed relationship to succeed. Before you and your mate commit to each other, you must each be able to apologize and forgive.

You hear a lot about forgiveness these days. That's because experts know anger is a poison that can ruin your health, as well as the health of your relationship. Practicing forgiveness, however, means more than saying the words. It means letting go of any anger you might have about a situation. If you've gone into your relationship consciously, understanding both your partner's strengths and weaknesses, forgiveness will come more easily. Often, our anger comes from the disappointment that our mate is not what we would like them to be in a particular instance.

Sharon and Philip had been engaged for several years. They were putting off marriage until they were both well-established in their careers. As time went by, Sharon found more and more occasions to be angry at Philip for not asserting himself with his family. It made her angry that he was always willing to be there for his widowed mother and his younger brother and sister. She felt they were taking advantage of Philip. Sharon was very close to calling their engagement off, when she came to me after a lecture and asked for advice. I asked her what it was about Philip that had first attracted her. She thought for a while before answering me, and with her words came the dawn of understanding. "I fell in love with Philip because of his kindness and supportive ways," she said.

Once Sharon understood that she was angry at Philip for being the person she had fallen in love with, she was able to forgive him. Although Philip had done nothing he needed to be forgiven for, Sharon needed to forgive him in order to heal her anger.

There are other times when your partner does something that disappoints you or lets you down. He forgets your anniversary or she doesn't call to let you know she'll be late coming home from work. When things like this happen, it's important to let the other person know how you feel. Tell him you're hurt that he forgot your anniversary. Tell her you were worried about her and that made you angry. Then, when he or she has apologized, forgive him or her and let it go. A committed relationship requires the ability to share your feelings honestly, and it requires forgiveness. Hanging on to anger, beating a dead horse, or never letting your mate forget his or her mistakes will kill the love in your relationship very quickly.

To be forgiven, you must be able to apologize. If you can't admit your mistakes without being defensive, you'll never be able to leave them behind. On the other hand, to apologize, you must feel safe. One of the reasons so many people have trouble apologizing is because they don't think their apology will be accepted. When you know your mate has a forgiving heart, it is much easier to say you're sorry. By the same token, it is easier to forgive someone who can admit their mistakes easily than it is to forgive someone who refuses to apologize.

The relationships in which forgiveness is readily given are the ones that withstand the test of time, hardship, and struggle. If you and your mate get in the habit of practicing forgiveness, you'll be able to handle any obstacle that comes your way.

Paul and Sheila had been dating for two years when Paul lost another job. In the last four years, he had been unemployed twice. Both times his company downsized and Paul's position was eliminated. Right before the holidays, Paul's latest employer was bought out by a huge conglomerate and he was without a job again.

When Paul heard the news he was so devastated he couldn't bear to tell his girlfriend. Several days went by, and Paul still couldn't bring himself to tell Sheila he was losing his job.

Even after his job ended, Paul left the house each morning as if he were going to work, but instead he went to a coffee shop in the next town. He'd spend the morning drinking coffee and reading the paper, then spend the afternoon walking the streets or sitting on a bench in the park. He couldn't face his girlfriend with more bad news.

After a few weeks, a friend of Sheila's spotted Paul walking around the park and called to tell her about it. Sheila knew something had to be wrong, so she drove over to the park and found Paul sitting on a bench staring into space. When she walked up to him, Paul was horrified.

He knew he had been caught and had to tell the truth. His heart ached for having not told Sheila the truth before. With tears spilling from his eyes, Paul asked Sheila to forgive him for not telling her right away. He told her he felt as bad about hiding the news from her as he did about losing his job.

Paul hadn't even finished his story before Sheila wrapped him in her arms and told him she forgave him. As hard as the last few years had been for them, they had always talked to each other from their hearts. There hadn't been any hardship too difficult for them to handle because they were always quick to apologize and quick to forgive.

If you're not ready to make apologies and forgive in your relationship, you're not ready for a serious commitment. Whether you and your mate date for one year or several years, use this time to practice these two skills before you even consider spending the rest of your lives together.

During the three years that Ursula and Larry dated they had many arguments and conflicts. Not once during that time did either of them apologize to the other after a fight. The tension between them would eventually subside, but the anger always bubbled just below the surface, ready and waiting to erupt during the next argument.

Eventually, so much resentment had built up from their many unresolved conflicts, that their relationship collapsed. Ursula and Larry broke up and went their separate ways without ever understanding that their biggest problem was they had never learned to forgive.

A COMMITMENT IS FOREVER

While all the things I've talked about in this chapter are important, the single most critical element of a successful relationship is the attitude with which you enter a lifelong commitment. For your relationship to last a lifetime, you must assume that it will.

How you visualize your relationship is exactly how it will evolve. If there is a mental escape clause in your commitment contract, your relationship will surely fail. If you cling to the notion that you can always leave if things don't go well, I can guarantee that things won't go well. On the other hand, if you see yourself spending the rest of your life with your partner, working through your problems together, getting help if you need it, and constantly striving to improve your relationship, you're creating the blueprint for a long, fulfilling life together.

Whether you commit to a new career, to being a parent, or to sharing the rest of your life with someone, making a commitment is a serious decision. Before you make it, be sure you're ready.

CHAPTER 9: TAKE ACTION

Committing to a lifelong relationship is not something to be taken lightly. There are many steps in arriving at the decision to spend the rest of your life with someone. Before you make that decision, you need to take a careful and honest look at yourself and your readiness.

1. Openness and honesty are critical in a successful relationship. In your journal, list everything about yourself that you would want your lifelong partner to know.

2. Your relationship deserves as much dedication as your career. Circle each of the actions you are willing to take to keep your relationship dynamic and alive.
   - Read books
   - Listen to tape programs
   - Watch video programs
   - Participate in workshops, seminars, or retreats
   - Seek professional counseling

3. Like a garden, your relationship needs to be nurtured to thrive. Circle each of the ways you would be willing to nurture your relationship.
   - Give your mate a 5-second compliment every day
   - Give your mate a 10-second kiss every day
   - Give your mate a 20-second hug every day
   - Have a 30-minute talk with your mate every day
   - Have a date night once a week
   - Have an overnight stay at a hotel once a month
   - Take a week-long vacation with just your mate, once a year

4. The single most critical element of a commitment that will last a lifetime is your attitude about it. In your journal, describe in detail your vision of your relationship.

Whether you decide you are ready for a commitment or not, you have learned some valuable things about yourself and relationships in this chapter. Keep your vision firmly in mind and never give up your goal of a lifetime of happiness with your perfect partner, whether this is the one or not.

Remember, whatever you sincerely believe, ardently desire, and enthusiastically act upon must inevitably come to pass.

CHAPTER 10

51 Ways to Meet Your Perfect Mate

ROMANCE ON ROUTE 66

When I meet someone for the first time, I always ask if they're in a relationship, and if so, how they met their partner. I love hearing the stories, and if I've learned anything over the past eighteen years it's that the possibility of meeting your perfect mate exists wherever you go. People have met their mate in every place imaginable, and even in some that are unimaginable.

For example, who would ever believe you could meet your mate while you're in your car, driving on the freeway at 65 miles per hour? I know of at least one couple that met that way, and there are probably others I haven't heard about.

Judy was a gorgeous blonde with a personality so big it extended beyond the confines of her car and into the atmosphere. When Cliff saw her driving along next to him on the freeway, he knew instantly that he had to meet her. He gave a polite honk on his horn and when she glanced his way, he smiled and waved. There was something appealing about Cliff, so Judy smiled back and then turned her eyes back to the road as she concentrated on her driving.

Cliff drove next to Judy for thirty-five miles, through three counties and two freeway changes. During this time, Judy enjoyed the flirtation and had a sense that it was quite harmless. When she finally came to her exit, she gave a little beep and a good-bye wave, and left the freeway. To her surprise, Cliff followed her and after they had both made their turn onto a surface street, he caught up to her and waved her over.

I know this sounds risky, but it happened more than twenty-five years ago, at a time when it was much safer to take a chance like this.

Judy pulled over and Cliff parked behind her. He got out of his car and approached the driver's side of Judy's car. When Judy rolled down her window, Cliff stuck out his hand and introduced himself. He was very flattering. He told Judy she was beautiful, that he'd fallen in love with her smile and he knew they were meant for each other. Of course, Judy took it all with a grain of salt, but she enjoyed Cliff's compliments and trusted him enough to join him for coffee at a nearby restaurant.

After talking for hours, Judy knew Cliff was right. They were meant for each other. They were married six months later, and they've been partners in love and in business for the past twenty-five years.

I tell you this story simply to prove you never know when you will meet your perfect mate. I would never recommend putting yourself in harm's way by meeting someone in this manner.

Most of you will have a hard time imagining that the 1970s were so different from the 1990s, but they were. The streets were much safer then. Hitchhiking was an everyday occurrence, good Samaritans abounded, and meeting your mate on the freeway wasn't likely to be dangerous.

LOOKING FOR LOVE IN ALL THE RIGHT PLACES

Even though I'm going to tell you fifty-one ways to meet your mate, the most important message in this chapter is that it isn't necessary for you to do anything special to meet your perfect partner. What is necessary is that you be alert to the possibilities that exist as you go about your daily activities. Whenever you are someplace where there are other people, the possibility exists that your perfect partner is there too. Think of it. Right this very second your mate is out there somewhere, waiting to meet you. He is grocery shopping, she is walking her dog, he is getting his car repaired, she is working out at the health club. All you have to do to meet them is to get up, get out, and talk to people.

Remember, you have to take action. If you don't reach out and talk to someone, you'll never know if he or she is your potential mate. You certainly won't meet someone by sitting at home and wishing for it to happen. Use the skills you learned on how to approach people and the suggestions in this chapter and talk, talk, talk to everyone you meet.

A business card will make it easier to reconnect with people you have met and would like to see again. If your employer doesn't provide you with business cards, have them printed yourself. It doesn't cost a lot and they are a wonderful way to make a lasting impression. When you meet someone you'd like to see again, it's nice to be able to give them your card instead of rummaging around for a pen or writing your number on a scrap of paper or a napkin.

If you're not sure what to put on your card, you might pick one of your hobbies or interests and create a clever name to describe it. An antique collector's card said, "Attic Delights." A watch collector's said, "It's About Time." A pet lover's said, "Precious Pet Palace." An outdoor lover's card said, "Happy Camper." Not only did these people have a calling card, they had a conversation starter as well.

The following list of fifty-one ways to meet your mate are meant to stimulate you to break out of your shell and wake up to the opportunities around you. Not all of them will be appropriate for you, but read each one and think about how it might apply in your life. If you approach your life with the attitude that anything can happen, anything can.

BE A GOOD CITIZEN AND APPEAR FOR JURY DUTY

The next time you get a summons for jury duty, don't ask to be excused. Go for it. Waiting to be called to sit on a jury is a perfect opportunity to meet people. Sometimes you have to wait days before you're selected to sit on a case. While you have nothing to do and nowhere to go, you might as well make the most of your time. Notice what other people are doing as they wait to be called and strike up a conversation around whatever it is they're doing, whether it's reading, knitting, or balancing their checkbook.

That's how Joe met Linda. For three days, Joe sat near her and secretly watched as she worked on the daily crossword puzzle. On the third day, Joe mustered up the courage to tell her he also enjoyed doing crossword puzzles and asked if he could help. Linda had been aware that Joe was watching her and was glad when he finally approached her. She was happy to share the puzzle with him and as they worked together to solve some of the more difficult clues, they exchanged small talk and began to get acquainted. At the end of the day, they agreed to meet for breakfast early the next morning.

The friendship that began as they waited to be called for jury duty developed into a love relationship and eventually resulted in marriage. When Joe and Linda got married, their wedding invitations were in the form of a crossword puzzle.

2

TALK TO PEOPLE WHEN YOU'RE ON A PLANE

Instead of burying your head in a book or catching up on paperwork when you fly, get to know the person sitting next to you. When I travel for my speaking engagements, I always take the opportunity to talk to my seatmates. A good way to start a conversation is to ask if your seatmate lives in the city you're leaving or the city you're flying to.

People tend to share a lot about themselves when they fly, probably because they think they'll never see you again, but if they happen to be your perfect mate, they'll be in for a bit of a surprise, won't they?

Kurt noticed that the woman seated next to him on his flight out of Chicago seemed really nervous during take-off. Her hands were clutching the armrests and her eyes were squeezed shut. Kurt asked if this were her first time flying, and Jackie told him she had been afraid to fly since she was a child. Jackie's disclosure opened up a discussion about their deepest fears and how they'd overcome them. It lasted for the rest of the flight. Although they were total strangers when they sat down on the plane, they left feeling like friends. While they were waiting to pick up their luggage at the baggage carousel, they exchanged phone numbers and Kurt called Jackie soon after for a date. Their subsequent romance was no fly-by-night affair, but a relationship that led to a lasting marriage.

3

CARRY OR WEAR SOMETHING PEOPLE WILL NOTICE

When I was a little girl, I had a shirt that looked like a newspaper. It had headlines and news print all over it. I loved that shirt. Everywhere I went, I got attention and compliments.

One of the easiest ways to meet people is to wear or carry something unique that others will notice and comment on. It must be something unusual that will attract attention and make you approachable.

For instance, a book with an eye-catching title such as, *Light His Fire: How to Keep a Man Hopelessly and Passionately in Love With You,* or *Light Her Fire: How to Ignite Passion and Excitement in the Woman You Love,* would be a good conversation starter. A stranger might say, "That's an interesting title. Does it work?" And you could answer, "I don't know. I don't have anyone to try it out on right now, but it's very interesting." Of course you don't have to choose my books, but you get the point.

When someone has the courage to approach you and begin the conversation, invite them in by sharing a little about why you chose the book and what you hope to get out of it. Don't make them feel as if they're intruding by responding abruptly.

Your eye-catching article doesn't have to be a book. It could be a souvenir T-shirt, a unique pin, a button, a cap, an old college sweatshirt, a necklace, suspenders—anything that makes you stand out from the crowd.

Make it a habit to notice details about other people. When you notice someone carrying or wearing something unique, ask them about it. Once you start looking, you'll be surprised how many things you'll find to comment on and it's a natural way to begin a conversation.

Sean was Scottish and proud of it. He always wore a pin that was embellished with his clan's coat of arms. Whether he wore it on his shirt, his sweater, or his coat, he made sure it was always visible and not a day would go by without someone asking him about his pin. However, when she saw his pin, Catherine didn't ask him what it meant: she told him.

Catherine, who was also Scottish, was the owner of a store that specialized in Scottish imports. The day that Sean discovered Catherine's store he was ecstatic. Not only did he find a source for some of his favorite food items, he found the mate he had been hoping to meet. Catherine and Sean dated for over a year, and when they got married Sean wore his kilt and their wedding procession was led by bagpipers.

WHEN YOU'RE AT THE GROCERY STORE, SHOP FOR MORE THAN JUST FOOD

The supermarket is a very logical place to meet the man or woman of your dreams. After all, everyone has to eat. I'll bet you've passed someone in the bakery section that you thought looked delicious but didn't know how to get them to jump into your cart.

When you see someone who looks interesting, nod and smile as you pass them in the aisle. Then, pay attention to where they go. This might be the perfect time for you to go there as well.

If you happen to see someone interesting while you're waiting in line at the service deli, check out what they have in their cart. Pick an item that lends itself to discussion and say something like, "Excuse me, I noticed you're buying french bread. What do you think of the bakery department here?" When they order, notice what they are buying and ask for their recommendation. For example, if they're buying sliced turkey, you could ask them which kind they would suggest. There are so many different choices—salt-free, fat-free, smoked, baked, broiled, shaved—that your question will be perfectly understandable.

Another way to start a conversation with someone you find interesting is to try to stand behind them in the checkout line. To start a conversation you could, once again, comment on something they have in their cart. If their cart is very full, you could help them put the groceries on the conveyor belt. They'll appreciate your kindness. Once you strike up a conversation, you might ask if they shop at that store often, and what time they think is the best time to shop. Who knows, running into them at the supermarket could become a habit!

When Jeff saw his future wife in the frozen food aisle, he didn't waste any time making his move. Hope was rubbing her hands together vigorously and Jeff thought she looked cold, so as he passed her he said, "They should install a heating system in this aisle." Hope looked up, smiled, and said, "You're not kidding." A few minutes later, Jeff saw Hope again in another aisle, looking at bottled water. He stopped next to her and asked her which bottled water she liked the best, saying he had recently decided to stop drinking the city water. They spent a few minutes talking about the benefits of having a water filter installed at home versus buying bottled water, then each of them continued with their shopping. The following week they saw each other again. The third time they met in the grocery store, Jeff asked Hope if she would like to join him for a drink sometime. Hope accepted, and after their engagement, Jeff told everyone he got his future wife at the supermarket.

VOLUNTEER TO HELP WITH A CHARITY EVENT

People love to come together for a good cause. Walkathons, telethons, auctions, dances, dinners, plays—the list of fundraising events organized to benefit charities is long.

Walkathons are especially popular. There are many opportunities to get to know people as you walk to raise money for such causes as AIDS, diabetes, or cancer research. The time everyone gathers before the event, the time spent walking, and the closing ceremonies at the end of the event are all times when people are feeling open and approachable.

Having a common mission is a wonderful way to start a relationship because you already have a shared interest. Cameron met Lucy at a walkathon for multiple sclerosis. They struck up a conversation at the registration table when Lucy complimented Cameron on his walking shoes and asked him what kind they were. They ended up walking together for the entire twelve miles and learned they both had family members suffering from multiple sclerosis. After the event they went out for pie together and their common bond became the foundation for a great relationship.

ATTEND A BOOK-SIGNING AT A BOOKSTORE OR LIBRARY

Bookstores provide a perfect opportunity for conversation and many even have a space where you can sit with a cup of coffee and a pastry as you plunge into your latest purchase. Many major bookstores schedule book-signings, where authors come to speak about and autograph their books. Since everyone at a book-signing is familiar with the author or the book, when you see someone you'd like to meet, you already have a conversation starter.

This is how Nancy met Tom. Nancy was an avid reader and attended book-signings at her local book store often. One time she spotted an interesting-looking man leaning against a bookshelf and as the author spoke, Nancy inconspicuously inched her way closer to him. When the lecture was over, Nancy worked her way into line behind Tom as he waited to get his book autographed. While they stood in line, Nancy asked Tom if he had read any of the author's previous books. During the ten minutes or so it took to get to the front of the line, Nancy and Tom learned enough about each other to realize they had a lot in common and wanted to talk more. Tom suggested they sit down in the reading area and continue their conversation. They talked for another hour and before they left, they exchanged phone numbers. Tom called Nancy a few days later and they began to write their own book of love.

7

TAKE AN ADULT EDUCATION CLASS

Adult education is big business. There are all sorts of classes available to anyone who is interested. Local colleges, community centers, the YMCA, proprietary schools—all offer classes of every kind and description. Whether you're interested in Chinese cooking, yoga, photography, scuba diving, antique collecting, computers, or golf, there is a class available. What better way to meet people with a common bond than in a class targeted specifically to your interest?

Joan met her mate at an eight-week square dance class. Joan had lost her first husband to cancer a few years before and felt it was time to get out and have some fun. She had square danced at a local park when she was a teenager and thought it was fun, so she decided to give it a try. She was happy when she found a class for singles and signed up right away.

Doug was also widowed. Recently he had been advised by his doctor to get out and get some exercise. Doug wasn't interested in running or bike riding, but he had always enjoyed dancing. Since he hadn't been dancing since his wife died, he wasn't sure how to get back into the swing of things. He knew he was too old for the nightclub scene, and in fact, he wasn't even sure if people danced in clubs anymore. He contacted his local senior center and learned that they sponsored a square dance class.

Doug signed up and by the second week he was "do-si-doing" with his future wife. Doug and Joan had so much fun together they joined a traveling square-dance club, and when they got married, instead of the music typical at wedding receptions, they had a square-dance band and caller.

TEACH AN ADULT EDUCATION CLASS

Whatever your expertise, your adult education center probably could use you as an instructor. Maybe you know a lot about auto mechanics, or computers, or cooking, or writing. As the teacher, you'll automatically get to know everyone in your class.

Will was an entrepreneur who was teaching a class on how to start a home-based business when he met Martha. She had taken the class because she wanted to open an upholstery business and run it out of her home. One night Martha stayed after class to ask Will for advice on how to market her business. As Will shared his expertise with Martha, he became aware that she was not only smart and ambitious, but also quite attractive. They sat in the classroom and talked until the school custodian kicked them out and then they continued their discussion as they walked around the block.

After the class ended, Will and Martha began dating. Martha's upholstery business was successful and so is the relationship that started nineteen years ago when Martha asked Will for extra help.

CHANGE YOUR MODE OF TRANSPORTATION

If you are in the habit of driving to work, try car pooling, taking the bus, or riding the subway for a change. You never know who you might meet when you leave your car at home and leave the driving to someone else.

Karen got tired of paying the high price of parking down-town and decided to use her city's transit system instead. She bought a month's pass and began riding the train to work. One morning the train car was more crowded than usual and Karen had to stand in the aisle. Suddenly she heard a man's voice say, "Excuse me, would you like to sit down?" A very attractive man stood and gave Karen his seat. Earl stood in the aisle next to Karen and they began talking. They discovered they worked in the same office building. Earl and Karen walked together from the station to work, and before they went their separate ways inside the building, they agreed to meet at the train stop the next morning. They began to meet at the station every day, chat during the ride, and then walk to work together. By the end of the first week, Karen and Earl had become close friends and they began dating soon after.

BECOME A VOLUNTEER USHER AT ONE OF THE THEATERS IN YOUR CITY

You may not be aware of it, but the ushers you see at concerts and plays are not employees of the theater. They are volunteers who have an interest in live performances and have offered to usher in exchange for the opportunity to watch the play or lis-ten to the concert. As an usher, not only do you get to see wonderful performances at no cost, you come in contact with thousands of people. You never know who you might meet as you hand out programs and direct people to their seats.

Don was a businessman who had majored in theater in col-lege. After he graduated, he missed the theater. He wanted to be involved somehow, even if only in a small way, and he decided to usher at one of the theaters in his area.

One night during intermission Don spotted a striking woman, standing alone in the theater lobby. He watched a while to see if she was waiting for someone, and when no one joined her he walked over and asked her how she was enjoying the play. Elaine responded with a thoughtful and insightful analysis and Don knew he had found a kindred spirit. He learned that Elaine was a season subscriber and they spent the rest of the intermission talking about the shows that would be presented that season.

The next month Don watched for Elaine and was delighted when he saw her walk through the door. They had another lively discussion during the intermission and enjoyed talking to each other so much they agreed to continue their conversation over coffee that night after the performance. As they got better acquainted, they discovered they felt very comfortable with one another and when Don asked Elaine for a dinner date, she accepted. They were married a few years later, and now they have their own cast of characters to keep them entertained, except on those nights when they get a baby-sitter and have a night at the theater alone.

THROW A PARTY

As strange as it may sound, you can meet your mate right in your own backyard. Here's how. Plan a party and ask each of your friends to bring two or three of their friends—people you don't know—with them.

Carla invited all of her single friends to a party and asked them to bring any eligible men they knew. She made it clear to her women friends that the men they invited were not to be men they themselves were interested in dating. Not only did Carla meet more than twenty eligible men, so did her friends. More than one match was made that night.

To help break the ice and get everyone relaxed, Carla organized a game of charades. Carla and Brian were on the same team, and as they thought up names of books, songs, and movies to act out, she and Brian discovered they liked the same kind of music. When the game was over, Brian followed Carla to the kitchen and kept her company while she replenished the snack trays. While they were talking, they discovered that they had something in common besides music. The companies they worked for were competitors. Brian was a partner in an architectural firm and Carla was the financial manager for another architectural firm in the same area. They talked shop for hours and before Brian left that evening, he promised to call Carla later that week. They started dating and fell in love. Now Brian is designing their dream house—the one they plan to live in "happily ever after."

VOLUNTEER AT YOUR CHURCH

Places of worship always need people to help with things like greeting, taking the offering, or teaching Sunday school. Many churches have a fellowship hour after the service where coffee and snacks are provided. Because people love to gather wherever they smell coffee or see food, volunteering to help during fellowship hour is a guarantee to meet people.

When Denise signed up to be on the welcoming committee, she had no idea it would lead to marriage. She was stationed behind the literature table where she welcomed visitors, answered questions and directed them toward the refreshment table when a nice-looking man came over and handed her a cup of coffee and a doughnut. "I thought I'd return your gracious hospitality," he said. Denise was quite surprised by Chuck's gesture of friendship and told him so. He explained it was his first visit to the church, and when he saw Denise, he thought she looked like a person who would be willing to talk to a stranger. They visited for a while about Chuck's recent move from another city, what it was like to be the "new kid on the block," and how easy it was to meet new people at church. Denise told Chuck if he really wanted to get acquainted fast, he should volunteer for the welcome table and he agreed to help her the following week. He was as good as his word, and from then on the two of them were a team. Two years later Chuck and Denise were married at the church where they met.

JOIN A HEALTH CLUB

For many people, their health club is also their social club. If you like to exercise, join a health club that offers the type of exercise you prefer. Aerobics classes, exercise equipment, weight rooms, swimming pools and racquetball courts are some of the amenities you'll find available, depending on which health club you choose.

Visit your club on different days of the week and at different times to get an idea of who visits the club, and when. For example, you'll find a different crowd early in the morning than you will on the weekends or in the evening. Talk to everyone you meet as you try the different classes and exercise machines.

When you lift weights or use the machines, it helps to have a partner. If you see someone interesting and they are not already working with someone, ask them to work out with you. You never know, your workout partner could become your life partner.

Dana joined a health club to get in shape and ended up not only losing weight, but gaining a husband. She met him the very first time she went to the club. Lou, who was on the machine next to Dana's, watched as she tried to figure out how to work her step machine. Seeing how frustrated she was, he offered to program her machine to the speed she wanted. As they exercised, Dana and Lou talked about their goal to lose weight. They both decided it would be easier to stay motivated with a partner to work out with and compare notes on their progress. They agreed to meet at the step machines the next day. After about a week of working out together, Lou invited Dana to a game of racquetball. She accepted and they've been playing together ever since.

GET INVOLVED IN A COMMUNITY THEATER

Even though you may not want to be on stage, community playhouses always need people to help with costumes, props, lighting, or in the box office. By the time the run of a show is over, the cast and crew feel a special connection with each other. Many lasting friendships, as well as marriages, have resulted from involvement in a theater production.

Laurie and Mark met at their community playhouse, where Mark had the lead and Laurie was the stage manager. Every Saturday night, the cast and crew went out for dinner after the show. During the ten weeks the show was in production, Mark and Laurie got to know each other in a group setting. The last night of the show, Mark asked Laurie for a date. For a change of scene, they took a bike ride on the beach and had a great time. Now Mark and Laurie have new roles as husband and wife.

ENJOY YOUR FAVORITE SPORT

The best way to meet someone while you enjoy your favorite sport is to join a team or a club. Ski clubs, golf clubs, dive clubs, bowling leagues, softball teams—whatever sport you love will have an organization you can join so you can enjoy it with others.

When Frank bought a sailboat and joined the sailing club at the marina where he docked his boat, he never imagined he'd meet a woman he could enjoy sailing with. He didn't think of sailing as a woman's sport.

One of the club's biggest activities was racing. The first race Frank participated in was as a crew member on another boat. That's where he met Julie, who was also a crew member. Frank and Julie spent three hours that day working side-by-side trying to win the race. Although they didn't come in first, they knew they had worked well together.

After crewing together in several more races, Frank invited Julia to join him on a sunset cruise. Since then, their relationship has been a breeze!

WALK THE DOG

Pets are notorious for bringing people together. Walking your dog is a great way to meet people, especially if you put an unusual collar or bandanna around the dog's neck. If you don't have a dog to walk, take yourself for a walk and approach other people who are out walking their dogs. It's an easy way to start a conversation and who knows? The dog you meet might end up being yours—along with its owner, of course.

Sarah made it a habit to walk her dog every day when she got home from work. Sport was a big yellow Labrador who wore a bandanna around his neck bearing the logo of the city's baseball team. As Sarah and Sport walked around the neighborhood, people would often chuckle and say, "I see your dog's a fan."

One evening, as Sarah and Sport took their exercise, Sarah noticed an attractive man jogging across the street from her. He was wearing a baseball cap with the city's team logo on it. Sarah and Sport crossed the street so they could pass the jogger and say hello. He smiled and acknowledged her team spirit with a "thumbs-up" as he jogged by.

When Sarah and Sport went for their walk the next day, Sarah took the same route as before, hoping to see her jogger again. Sure enough, she passed him at almost the exact spot where she had seen him the day before. This time, the man stopped to pet Sport and to comment on the bandanna. He introduced himself as Daryl.

Daryl and Sarah saw each other several times during the next few weeks and eventually they began to feel like friends. Finally Daryl invited Sarah to a baseball game and they've been dating ever since.

VISIT AN ART GALLERY

Art lovers, by nature, tend to be romantics. As someone once said, "Art is the accomplice of love." Starting a conversation with someone you find interesting in an art gallery or museum should be easy. Find a way to approach him or her and look for an opportunity to make a comment or ask a question about a piece of art that you are both observing at the same time.

As Rick was strolling through a modern art exhibit one day, he saw Sharon carefully studying a metal sculpture and thought, "That woman is far more beautiful than anything on exhibit here."

Rick stopped to study the sculpture too. After a moment, he turned to the woman and said, "What do you think this represents?" Sharon gave her interpretation and asked Rick what he thought. Rick responded that he thought it looked like a bird in flight and it represented freedom to him. They talked a little more about the sculpture and then moved on to the next work. They again shared their thoughts and interpretations and before they knew it, they had gone through the entire gallery together.

When they finished touring the gallery, Rick and Sharon weren't ready to say good-bye and decided to go for a cup of coffee and some more conversation. They soon discovered they shared many common interests. Besides a love of art, they were both concertgoers and accomplished musicians. Rick played the flute in an amateur chamber orchestra and Sharon played the violin in a string quartet. They quickly became a duet and when they got married, their wedding reception was held at the art gallery where they first met and the music was provided by Sharon's string quartet.

CANCEL YOUR NEWSPAPER SUBSCRIPTION

I'm not suggesting that you stop reading the paper, just that you buy it at the newsstand instead of having it delivered. The ritual of walking to the newsstand, buying your paper, and scanning the front page while you sip your cappuccino or latte is a nice way to start the day.

George had been buying his newspaper at a newsstand instead of having it delivered to his house for a couple of weeks when he met Sally. He was standing there reading the headlines when he heard Sally talking to the vendor about the front-page story, a dramatic fall in the stock market. George slowly inched his way closer and added a comment to their discussion. Soon he and Sally were involved in an intense conversation about the economy. During the discussion George learned that Sally was a stockbroker. George introduced himself, adding that he was a professor of economics at the university. After talking for a few minutes, they each went their separate ways. A few mornings later they saw each other again at the newsstand and continued their conversation of the previous day.

They continued to see each other frequently while they were buying their morning paper, and at some point they moved from discussing the economy to discussing their work and their personal lives. When George invited Sally for dinner at a local up-scale restaurant, she accepted. They had a wonderful time, and today their discussions are often about how to invest their "mutual" funds.

GO TO THE LAUNDROMAT

Nobody ever said doing the laundry is fun, but if you have to do it, it's a lot more interesting to go to a laundromat than it is to do it alone in your basement or laundry room. There are people in the laundromat at all hours of the day or night, and it's always easy to start a conversation. If you see someone you want to talk to, you can ask something as simple as which dryers work best, what detergent they use, or just open with a comment on how boring laundry can be.

Jack will never forget the day he met his future wife at the laundromat. It was late Saturday afternoon, and he had just finished loading his clothes into the washer when he looked up to see a pretty brunette wearing cutoffs and a tie-dyed T-shirt struggling to open the door. She was carrying a laundry basket piled high with clothes. Seizing the opportunity, Jack ran over to open the door for Susan. He then took his chivalry one step further and offered to carry her heavy load to the washers for her. Susan thanked Jack profusely and after she had gotten her clothes separated and into the machines, she joined Jack where he was sitting and they talked while they waited for their clothes to wash and dry. Jack noticed that Susan had so much laundry it took three machines to hold it all and he assumed she must be doing wash for her family. When Jack asked Susan how many children she had, she started to laugh. She told him she was single with no children, she just hated going to the laundromat so much that she had put it off for three weeks. Jack was surprised at how relieved he was to learn she was single. They talked some more while they folded their clothes and Jack helped Susan carry her basket to her car. Before he left, he said he hoped he would't have to wait three weeks to see her again.

Next Saturday, Jack returned to the laundromat on the same day and at the same time, hoping to see Susan again. She was there and greeted Jack as an old friend. This time, before Susan left, Jack got her phone number and they began dating a few weeks later. Now that they're married, Susan doesn't mind doing the laundry, because she has Jack to keep her company.

TAKE A CRUISE

I can't think of a more romantic way to meet a mate than on a cruise. A cruise is a wonderful way to meet people, especially if you book one that's geared for singles. You can spend as much or as little as you wish for a cruise. They come in a wide range of prices. You can take an inexpensive, three-day cruise and have just as much fun as you would on a cruise around the world. You will meet people by the pool, in the casino, in the dining room, at the midnight buffet, on the dance floor, or in an exercise class.

Bob met Jennifer on a five-day cruise to the Bahamas. One evening, Bob was playing the quarter slot machines in the casino when he hit a $1,000 jackpot. Jennifer, who was sitting at the slot machine next to him, was so excited about Bob's good fortune, that she began chatting with him animatedly while Bob waited for the attendant to turn off his light and give him his voucher. She was so impressed with Bob's luck that she sat next to him while they played blackjack, roulette, and craps.

Bob was charmed by Jennifer's easy banter and open personality, and they ended the evening with a moonlight walk around the deck. As they walked and talked, they were shocked to discover they lived just a short, two-hour drive from one another.

The day they came ashore to fly home, they promised to stay in touch and it wasn't long before they were making the two-hour commute to each other's homes on a regular basis. Eighteen months later Bob and Jennifer were on another cruise—this time a honeymoon cruise to the Greek Isles.

21

ENROLL IN BIBLE STUDY OR A SPIRITUAL CLASS

There's a reason why so many people have met their mate at church, at temple, or at a spiritual retreat center. No matter what your religious beliefs are, studying and discussing spiritual issues offer you an opportunity to relate to others on a deeper level than you otherwise might in your daily life. When you meet someone in this setting, you already have the basis for an enduring and deep relationship.

When Chet enrolled in a Bible study program at his church, he was a little nervous. The last time he had studied the Bible was as a child in Sunday school and he wasn't sure what to expect. He needn't have worried. The minister who conducted the classes was a strong leader who knew how to provoke stimulating discussion. To encourage everyone's participation, he divided the class into several small groups which he presided over at different times during the class. Chet was assigned to Charlene's group.

Charlene welcomed Chet warmly and took charge of introducing him to the other group members and making him feel at home. Over the next few weeks, Chet was continually impressed with Charlene's deep faith and realized he was falling in love with her.

They began dating, and their relationship deepened as their love grew. By the time they were married, two years later, Chuck had become a lay minister and their church became the cornerstone of their life together.

GO SHOPPING

Some people love shopping, some people hate it, but we all have to do it at some time or another. No matter how you feel about it, a shopping trip can become another chance to meet your mate if you will just look at it a little differently.

Whenever possible, shop at a store that sells items that would interest a member of the opposite sex. For instance, if you're a man, the next time you need a gift for your mother, your sister, or a friend, shop at a store that specializes in cosmetics, perfume, or women's clothing instead of buying a gift certificate at a large department store. A woman who needs a gift for a man might shop at a sporting goods store, a hardware store, or an electronics store.

Look for opportunities to ask other shoppers their opinion. People love being asked for their advice and it's a great way to start a conversation. For example, if you're shopping for a gift for your sister and you see a woman who interests you, ask her to help you select coordinates that work well together. If you're in a hardware store and you see an interesting-looking man, ask him a question about plumbing or lighting.

Nadine went shopping at an electronics warehouse to look for speakers for her stereo, but there were so many speakers to choose from she was completely overwhelmed. She was about to ask a salesclerk for assistance when she noticed Dale, a very attractive man, standing a few feet away. She decided to ask his advice on which speakers would work best with her system.

Dale was very knowledgeable and could tell Nadine exactly which speakers were best for her purposes. Nadine was very grateful and complimented Dale on his expertise. They continued talking for a while and discovered they were both jazz lovers. Dale definitely struck a chord when he asked Nadine to meet him at a jazz fest the next evening, and they've been keeping time together ever since.

CHECK OUT THE LIBRARY

You can find a lot more at the library than just books. You can go to a lecture, visit an art exhibit, or join a book club. And, like a bookstore, libraries have the perfect conversation starters: books, magazines, and even videos. In Kathy's case, she even found a mate.

Kathy had gone to the library almost every Saturday since she was a small child. One of her fondest memories was the day she finally mastered writing her name so she could qualify for a library card of her own. One Saturday morning, Kathy was in the checkout line at the library when she noticed the man in front of her was carrying a book she had just finished reading. She leaned forward to tell him how much she had enjoyed it, and they started talking about their love of reading. They became so engrossed in their conversation that they sat outside on a bench until the library closed talking about reading and the many ways books had enhanced their lives.

Seth and Kathy's first love may have been reading, but they found lasting love with each other. They've been married seventeen years and they take their children to the library every Saturday morning, just as Kathy's father had taken her.

24

EAT LUNCH OUT

If you're in the habit of eating lunch at the same place every day, it's time to get out of your rut. Instead of eating at your desk or in the company cafeteria, get out and explore the neighborhood where you work. Try the neighborhood diner one day, an upscale restaurant another, and an ethnic restaurant still another. If there's a park nearby, pack your lunch and eat there occasionally.

When Bill decided to change his routine, he was only looking for a change of scene, not a wife. But a wife was what he got.

It seemed to Bill that he had been eating lunch at his desk forever. One day he realized what a rut he was in and decided to go out for lunch. He enjoyed it so much he never ate at his desk again. Bill was lucky. There was an abundance of restaurants in the area where he worked, and he was able to enjoy a variety of foods; but the day he met Betsy at an Italian restaurant, pasta became his favorite dish. Betsy was his waitress and unlike most of the waitresses Bill encountered on his lunch-hour wanderings, she gave him a friendly smile, in spite of being very busy. Bill returned to the restaurant again and again just to see Betsy smile as she poured his coffee or served his meal. Finally, Bill asked Betsy for a date. She accepted, and Bill took her to a hockey game, thinking that it would be a nice change of scene for Betsy, who spent all day around food. Betsy was impressed with his thoughtfulness and they had a fabulous time. They fell in love and were married later that year, all because Bill got out of his lunch-hour rut.

VISIT A VIDEO STORE

A video store is great place to browse for interesting people at the same time you are browsing for a movie. Within the breast of most movie fans beats the heart of a closet critic. If you see someone you'd like to meet while you're in the video store, ask them what they think of a particular movie. They'll probably be glad to review it for you.

That's how Shelly and Bernie met. Shelley had picked up a newly released comedy and was trying to decide whether to rent it or not. She looked up from reading the summary on the back of the box and saw Bernie standing nearby, so she asked him if he had seen the movie. When he saw what movie she was holding, he started to laugh. As he told Shelly about the movie, Bernie laughed harder and harder. Bernie's laughter was contagious, and soon Shelly was laughing right along with him. When they finally stopped laughing long enough to introduce themselves, they discovered they lived on the same street.

They left the video store together and decided to have a cup of coffee at the coffee shop next door. They liked each other very much and began dating. Laughter brought Bernie and Shelly together, and laughter is still at the heart of their relationship after seven years of marriage.

TAKE DANCE LESSONS

Ballroom, swing, disco, country-western, folk dancing, tap dancing, jazz—take your pick. Dance lessons are a great way to meet a mate. In addition, if you learn ballroom dancing, you'll be gaining an important social skill that will provide you with hours of fun and take you from wallflower to belle of the ball in a short period of time. After dance lessons, you won't have to sit and tap your foot while everyone else dances the night away. When someone asks you to dance, you'll be able to say, "I'd love to," and mean it.

When Samantha was asked to be the maid-of-honor at her best friend's wedding, her excitement was dampened by her fear of getting out on the dance floor. She resolved to learn some basics before the wedding, so she signed up for a ballroom dance class.

At the wedding reception, Samantha was really glad she had taken lessons when an extremely handsome man asked her to dance. Instead of having to turn him down, she was able to glide around the floor with him as if they had danced together all their lives. They barely sat down for the rest of the evening. Samantha felt like a princess who had finally met Prince Charming as Aaron spun her around and around and her long gown billowed behind her.

Fortunately for Aaron, Samantha didn't turn into a pumpkin at midnight, just an attractive woman who had changed into a pair of jeans before driving home from the reception. Aaron and Samantha's fairy tale romance was complete when they danced at their own wedding a few years later.

JOIN A PROFESSIONAL ORGANIZATION

Most professions have organizations affiliated with them that provide education, support, and networking. Active involvement in such an organization is sure to provide you with the opportunity to meet other people with a common interest. The best way to get to know people in any organization is to be an officer or board member or to work on a committee.

When Janet joined a professional association it was to advance her career, but the benefit to her personal life proved to be far more important.

Janet was a motivational speaker who belonged to a national speaker's association. She was a member of a local chapter and attended dinner meetings once a month. Twice a year she went to the association's national convention where she met people from all over the country.

One year Janet's local chapter hosted the convention. It was there that she met Ray, who belonged to a chapter in another state. During the two-day convention, Janet and Ray became friends and Janet gave Ray a tour of her city before he left for home. They stayed in touch, and their long-distance relationship grew stronger and stronger over the next three years. Eventually, Ray found an apartment in Janet's city and moved there to be closer to her. Shortly after that, he proposed to Janet and they were married nine months later. Now, Janet and Ray keep each other motivated as they work on renovating the turn-of-the-century Victorian home they bought in the historical district of their city.

ATTEND A REUNION

When you receive an announcement about a reunion, whether it's a grade-school, high-school, or college reunion, go. Connect with as many people as you can, even those you didn't socialize with in school. People change. The class nerd is probably the CEO of a powerful corporation now, and the studious girl with the thick glasses may be a glamorous talk-show hosts, so don't limit yourself to hanging out with your old pals.

Even when he was in high school, Larry sensed that he was missing out on knowing a lot of interesting people, but he was so caught up in his role of captain of the football team that his friendships had been limited to other members of the football team and cheerleaders. When he went to his high-school reunion, he made it a point to seek out the people he hadn't known well in school.

Larry talked to a lot of people that night, but when he found Kate, who had been a member of the school orchestra, he stopped mixing and concentrated on her. She was stunning! Larry couldn't understand how he could have overlooked her beauty when they had been in school together. Larry asked Kate to dance, and they spent the rest of the evening laughing and talking as they reminisced about their high-school days.

After the reunion, Larry and Kate began dating and now call themselves high school sweethearts!

DO VOLUNTEER WORK FOR A PHILANTHROPIC
ORGANIZATION

There are so many organizations that need your help. The Juvenile Diabetes Foundation, the American Heart Association, the Cancer Society, the Society for Mental Retardation, are just a few. Besides national organizations, there are many groups at the local level that are dedicated to helping others. Volunteering your time, either as a committee member or in some other capacity, is a sure way to meet new people.

Jessica volunteered to help with a fund-raising ball for the Alzheimer's Association as chairperson of the welcoming committee. During the three months they were preparing for the event, she made many new friends but she met her best friend the night of the ball.

Jessica looked striking in her new evening gown, as she stood by the door, welcoming people and directing them to the main ballroom. Jessica felt as good as she looked that night and was aware of the many admiring looks directed her way. Jessica thought all the men looked gorgeous in their tuxedos, but when she spotted Ron her heart skipped a beat. He was movie-star handsome and when he gave her a huge smile and told her how lovely she looked, Jessica almost stopped breathing. She returned his smile, as she thanked him for the compliment and directed him to the ballroom. When he passed her, he told Jessica he hoped to see her later in the evening.

Jessica couldn't have agreed more.

When she was through with her welcoming duties and had joined the crowd in the main ballroom, Jessica's handsome man found her and asked her to dance. He introduced himself and they had a marvelous evening together talking and dancing the night away. Shortly after the ball, they began dating seriously. Jessica and Ron have been married ten years and have three beautiful children who keep them very busy, but they still donate their time to the Alzheimer's Association.

ATTEND FAMILY GET-TOGETHERS

Don't miss a family get-together because you think it'll just be old Uncle Charlie and Aunt Mabel or a bunch of little rug-rats. Family get-togethers are not just for family. Birthday, anniversary, engagement, and graduation celebrations provide a great opportunity to meet new people.

Jonathan met the love of his life at his brother's college graduation party. He expected a dull evening until he saw Shannon, a gorgeous blonde, standing by the buffet table, talking to another woman.

Jonathan approached the buffet table and took a plate. As he made his way around the table, selecting various dishes to sample, he seized the opportunity to ask Shannon how she knew his brother. She didn't. She had come to the party with a sorority sister who was a friend of Jonathan's brother. Their conversation shifted from Jonathan's brother to college life, and eventually led to where they could go to have a drink and talk privately.

That was twenty-eight years ago. Shannon and Jonathan now have a son and daughter of their own, both of whom will soon graduate from college.

ATTEND A WEDDING

Never miss a wedding if you can possibly help it. As it says on the invitation, your presence is an honor and your being there will help make the occasion perfect for the bride and groom. Besides, weddings are such happy occasions. Once the music starts, everyone is in a party mood.

Lynn met Ben at her brother's wedding. Ben had spent most of the evening watching Lynn, trying to see if she was with a date. Finally, about fifteen minutes before the band was scheduled to stop playing, Ben asked Lynn to dance. He had such a good time dancing with her he wished he had asked her earlier. After Lynn shook Ben's hand and thanked him for the dance, she turned to walk away. As he watched her move toward a crowd of guests, Ben acted on impulse and ran over to her and said, "Lynn, would you like to go to dinner and see a movie with me next weekend?" Without hesitation, Lynn said, "I'd love to."

Ben was flying high as he left the reception that night, but not nearly as high as on the day he and Lynn were married four years later.

WAIT A WHILE

We all spend a lot of time waiting: at the post office, at the bank, at a fast food restaurant, at the grocery store, or at the dentist's office. The next time you're waiting in line, use the time to meet someone new instead of wishing you were somewhere else.

That's what Harriet did while she waited in line to pick up her dry cleaning one day. When she overheard Charles, who was in the line next to her, tell the clerk he wanted a pair of pants altered, Harriet took the opportunity to ask him if he'd ever had his clothes altered there before. She explained that she had a skirt she needed shortened, and was looking for a place to have it done.

In the process of talking about their dry cleaning Harriet and Charles learned they were taking night classes at the same school. They finished picking up their cleaning at the same time and walked out together.

By the time they reached their cars, they had set a date to meet for coffee after school the next night. Waiting in line brought Harriet and Charles together and they've been together ever since.

GO TO THE COUNTY FAIR, AN AMUSEMENT PARK, OR A CARNIVAL

When people go to an amusement park or carnival, they tend to become more open and playful. When they're having fun riding the bumper cars or playing the ring toss game, they are more approachable than usual. Whether it's at a street fair or a state fair, it's easy to meet people in a setting where there is so much activity.

Ned and Suzanne met at the county fair. Ned was at the shooting gallery when he noticed a pretty young woman out of the corner of his eye. Aware that she was watching him, Ned worked really hard to score as many points as possible. His aim was to win a big, stuffed teddy bear.

From time to time, Ned would look over his shoulder and smile at the woman and she would smile back. When Ned won the teddy bear he walked over and handed it to Suzanne, saying, "Without your beautiful smile, I could never have won this. I want you to have it."

Suzanne was charmed and when Ned invited her to ride the Ferris wheel with him, she accepted.

Needless to say, they spent the rest of the day together at the carnival and began dating. Married eleven years, Suzanne's pet name for Ned is "Neddy the Teddy."

GET INVOLVED IN A PRETEND MURDER

In the last several years restaurants and theaters have begun offering what are called "Murder Mysteries." Audience participation is the key to their success. The actors set the scene and provide hints to help you figure out who killed whom with what instrument. As audience members search the area for clues, consult with each other about the evidence they've found, and speculate on the identity of the murderer, they can't help but get to know one another.

Danny may have been a little skeptical but he had never been to a murder mystery party, so he went with an open mind, ready to have fun. Everyone at his table was married except himself and a very attractive woman named Denise. Denise and Danny teamed up as they looked for clues to the murder and tried to solve the mystery. Danny and Denise had a marvelous time together as they looked for the murder weapon under seat cushions, in potted plants, and behind pictures.

They never did find the murder weapon, but they didn't care. They had found each other!

ATTEND A SCHOOL FUNCTION

Whether it's for your child or someone else's, school functions are a great way to meet people. Kids need all the support they can get for their football games, plays, and concerts, and attending them will help keep you young.

Paul's neighbor's son, Ian, had cut his grass for years. When Ian's basketball team went to the city championships, Paul was excited for Ian and decided to go the game and cheer him on. At the game Paul sat next to Ian's Aunt Julie. They were immediately attracted to each other, and during the game they stood shoulder to shoulder as they cheered wildly for Ian's team, which took the lead early, lost it, and then came from behind to win in the last two minutes of the game. Julie and Paul decided the win called for a victory celebration. They went out for a drink together and talked for hours.

Two years later their wedding was the happy cause for celebration.

SHOP FOR A CAR

Even if you're not in the market for a new car, comparison shopping at car dealerships will not only make you a better informed consumer when you are ready to buy a car, it could be the way to meet your mate. Visit as many dealerships as you have time for, and shop in the evenings as well as on weekends or during the daytime. Stay alert for an opportunity to approach someone who attracts you and ask for their opinion or advice about any cars they might be considering.

Although Andy's auto lease wasn't up for two years, he loved to look at cars in his spare time. He was an expert on the prices and features of different cars. One Saturday when he was looking at sports cars, he met Pam. When she saw Andy looking at a bright blue Miata convertible, she approached and asked if he thought it was a good car. She told him she couldn't decide between a Miata or a Fiat she had test driven the week before.

Andy, who currently drove a Miata, and had previously owned a Fiat, offered Pam some insights. She was impressed with his knowledge and spent an hour asking him questions. When they parted, Andy gave Pam his card and said he'd be happy to answer any more questions.

Three days later, Pam called and asked Andy if he would meet her at the dealership and test drive the Miata with her. He said he would be happy to.

Andy's knowledge of cars helped Pam make her decision and after she ordered the Miata with the options she wanted, she and Andy went out for a bite to eat to celebrate her new car.

Looking back on it, Pam says she fell in love with her car and husband on the same day.

VISIT THE BEACH

Even if you don't meet anyone, a day at the beach is always a treat. There are so many things you can do. Sunbathe, swim, body surf, jog, walk, build a sand castle, join in a volleyball game, play catch, fly a kite, just sit and relax—the list is endless. And, because it is so relaxing, people seem to be naturally friendly on a beach.

One Sunday afternoon, Doreen and her girlfriend took a Frisbee and went to the shore. When Doreen threw the Frisbee to her friend, it zigged when it should have zagged and landed on someone's towel. Embarrassed, Doreen ran over to get it and apologized to the occupant of the towel. She was a little startled when a very good-looking man with a gorgeous tan smiled up at her and said, "No problem."

Not two minutes later, Doreen threw the Frisbee again and it landed in almost the same spot as before. She was mortified as she ran to get it for a second time. Instead of giving it back, Matt offered to teach her how to throw it so that it went straight. By the time Doreen learned how to throw it, Matt had joined the game.

After they had worn themselves out playing Frisbee, Matt offered to buy Doreen and her friend a lemonade. The three of them sat and talked until it was time for Doreen and her girlfriend to leave. Before they left, they arranged to meet at the beach and play Frisbee again the next day after work.

When Doreen's girlfriend had to cancel, Doreen decided to go alone. She and Matt threw the Frisbee for a while, then sat and talked until it began to get cold. They went to dinner together and then later they took a moonlight walk along the beach. Their love for each other started that night and has grown and deepened with each year that has passed.

JOIN YOUR HIGH SCHOOL OR COLLEGE
ALUMNI ASSOCIATION

As a member of your alumni association, you'll be notified of homecoming activities and other alumni get-togethers.

When you attend these events, not only will you have an opportunity to get reacquainted with people from your graduating class, you'll meet people from other classes as well.

Shortly after Amanda joined her alumni association, she and her college roommate decided to attend homecoming weekend for the first time since they had graduated twenty years before. They went to the football game, the bonfire, and the dance afterwards.

It was while standing around the bonfire that Amanda recognized Sean, a man she remembered from her chemistry class. They had been lab partners during Amanda's senior year. Amanda was really happy to see Sean, who had been a good friend at the time and she hurried over to say hello. Sean was as happy to see Amanda as she was to see him. They talked by the bonfire for over an hour, catching each other up on their lives since college, and then decided to go into the gymnasium to dance. The next day, they went on the alumni hay ride together and had a great time. As the weekend came to a close, they swapped business cards and promised to stay in touch.

They did more than stay in touch, they got married and they've been together now for five years.

VOLUNTEER FOR A POLITICAL CAMPAIGN

Working on a political campaign is a great way to have fun while you support a candidate or cause you believe in. Whether you volunteer at the local, state, or national level, you'll be exposed to hundreds of new people who all have the same political beliefs you do. One of those people might be your perfect partner. When Daniel decided to join the campaign for a candidate running for state senator he never expected to find a running mate of his own.

Daniel thought he'd only be making some phone calls and passing out brochures, but as he became more involved, his enthusiasm led him to work twenty hours a week at campaign headquarters. One night, when he was making phone calls to raise funds for his candidate, he was seated next to Paula. Daniel soon discovered that Paula's enthusiasm matched his own. They spent many late nights working together at campaign headquarters. One night, Daniel suggested they take a break and grab a bite to eat at the all-night diner down the street.

For the first time since they had met, they talked about things other than the political campaign. They discovered they both loved opera, foreign films, and the outdoors. They made a date to see each other the following Saturday night, and began to date steadily.

Although their candidate lost the election, Daniel and Paula still felt like winners. They had won each other's hearts.

BE A COACH

Volunteer to be a coach and you can participate in your favorite sport, contribute to your community, and meet a lot of people in the process. Besides the players on the team, you'll get to know their friends and family when they come to watch the games.

When Norm volunteered to be one of the coaches for his nephew's hockey team, he never dreamed he'd meet his future mate at the ice rink. Four mornings a week, Norm had to be on the ice by 5:30. Most of the parents dropped their children off and went back to bed, but Norm noticed that one woman always stayed for the whole practice.

She was an attractive woman, and after three weeks Norm decided to introduce himself even though he assumed she was one of the parents and probably married. As it turned out, Barbara was a neighbor of one of the children on the team, and she was single. The parents of the child had unusual work schedules and, being a morning person, Barbara offered to take their son to hockey every day.

Barbara and Norm started chatting during all of the rest periods and when Norm noticed Barbara showing up at the games as well as the practices, he decided to ask her for a date. Knowing hockey was something they had in common, Norm took Barbara to a professional hockey game. That was fifteen years ago, and now Norm coaches their son's hockey team while Barbara cheers the team and cheers up the coach.

JOIN A SUPPORT GROUP

Whether you need support in handling an illness, an addiction, or a loss, there is probably a support group for you. Many of these groups have weekly meetings, as well as regional conferences several times a year. I can't think of a nicer way to meet someone than in a supportive, encouraging environment.

Alice and Craig met at a meeting of Alcoholics Anonymous. Alice had been sober for four years and Craig had been sober for five and they both took their responsibility to support newcomers very seriously. They always said hello at the coffee urn and made small talk after the meetings, but it wasn't until they were in the same discussion group that they got to know one another.

After several months of being in meetings together, Craig began to realize that not only did he see Alice as a close friend, he was also very attracted to her. He took her by surprise one evening when he asked her to join him for dinner. Less than a year later Craig proposed to Alice. The friendship that started in a support group became the foundation for the healthy loving relationship they have today.

GO TO A FLEA MARKET, ANTIQUE SHOW, OR OTHER LARGE SHOW

Flea markets, antique shows, home shows, outdoor recreation shows or other large exhibitions where people display their merchandise will put you in the middle of thousands of people. As you browse and barter your way from booth to booth, you'll meet a variety of people, one of whom might be your mate.

Liz had been at the antique show for hours, walking from one display to the next, looking at merchandise and talking to the vendors. Each person she met seemed to be nicer than the one before. Then she came to a booth with antique phonographs, something that Liz had always wanted.

She fell in love with one in particular and asked Jerry, the vendor, the price. When Jerry quoted the price, Liz ruled it out as much too expensive, but she lingered, longing to own this little gem. Although it was very old, it appeared to be in mint condition. After almost an hour of indecision, Liz finally decided to buy the phonograph she loved so much. Liz was delighted with her purchase and Jerry was delighted for her.

He loved antique phonographs as much as Liz did and was happy that one this special was going to a good home. They exchanged phone numbers and agreed that they would try to connect during the next antique show, which would be held in a month.

The following month, Liz went to the antique show, and found Jerry's booth. This time Liz spent most of her time talking with Jerry instead of looking at other booths. After a while, Jerry asked Liz to join him behind his booth and share the lunch he had brought.

For the next six months, Liz worked the antique shows with Jerry and they had so much fun together their working relationship became a love relationship. Now that they're married, they work side-by-side in the antique shop they own together.

43

SCOPE OUT THE BUILDING WHERE YOU WORK

Although you may not want to date a co-worker, if you work in a large office building there are probably lots of people outside your company that you could be your potential mate. Look at the directory in the lobby and learn who else shares space with you. Watch to see who comes out of what office. Learn a little bit about the other businesses so if you happen to run into someone from another company, you know enough about that company to strike up a conversation.

Joel's company was one of fifteen companies that occupied a multi-storied office building. One day, Joel noticed an exotic-looking woman go into an insurance company down the hall from his office. He saw her again a few days later, and then again the next day. By now he was intrigued and wanted very much to meet her. He asked several of his co-workers what they knew about the insurance company, and did some research of his own at the library. When he met Selva at the elevator one day, he had enough information about her company to have an interesting conversation. In fact, Selva was so impressed by how much Joel knew about the company she worked for she began asking him about his company.

Every time they bumped into each other in the hall, they picked up their conversation where they left off. After talking "shop" for a few weeks, Joel asked Selva for a date. She turned him down the first time; but he persisted, and when she said yes, Joel was ecstatic. He'd already fallen in love, but it took Selva several more months to return Joel's feelings. After three years of dating, they will be getting married this fall.

HAVE A HOME IMPROVEMENT PARTY

If your house needs to be painted, your garden needs to be planted, or you need a deck built, have a home improvement party. You provide the food and drinks and your friends provide the labor. Invite as many of your friends as possible, and ask them to bring as many friends as they can. You'll get a lot of work done and meet lots of new people.

When Betty, who was a single mom, bought her house, every room needed to be repainted. She couldn't afford to hire professionals to have the job done, so she invited a few of her closest friends, asked them to bring a few of their friends, and then ordered enough pizza to feed a battalion of house painters. By the time the day was over, her small army of workers had painted every room in the house, and had eaten enough pizza to support the local pizzeria for a week.

Not only did Betty get a freshly painted house that day, she also met her mate. Donald had come to the home improvement party with one of Betty's friends when the baseball game he had tickets for got rained out. With nothing better to do, he decided to go to the party. His decision gained him a wonderful wife and three great children.

GO ON A BLIND DATE

I believe blind dates are getting a bum rap! I'm convinced if someone were to conduct a survey, it would be proven that at least as many blind dates lead to romance as lead to disaster.

Stan's friend, Marty, kept talking about a woman he worked with who he thought would be perfect for Stan. Marty described Candice as an attractive, hard-working woman with a great sense of humor. Every time Marty suggested that Stan call Candice, Stan would say, "But I don't even know her!" Marty would always respond by saying, "So, get to know her."

After being badgered by Marty for four months, Stan finally called Candice and invited her to a basketball game. They met at the sports arena and felt a connection the moment they started talking. They missed the entire first half of the game, because they were so engrossed in conversation that they didn't even bother to go to their seats. Even after they sat down, they kept talking and didn't realize the game was over until they noticed everybody get up to leave.

Today, when they go to a basketball game, they never take their eyes off the court. But why would they? Their son is the center.

TAKE YOUR CAR TO THE DEALERSHIP FOR SERVICE

When you need your car serviced or repaired, don't just drop it off at the dealer. Take advantage of the comfortably furnished waiting rooms available at most dealerships and wait while they work on your car. You could write letters, balance your checkbook, catch up on your reading, or just watch TV while you wait, but don't forget to make friends with anyone interesting who is waiting with you.

Lorraine had taken her car in for routine service and was balancing her checkbook, when she became aware of an interesting-looking man sitting nearby. When they made eye contact, he commented that he was impressed with her dedication to her task and confessed he never balanced his checkbook. Lorraine was astonished anyone would neglect what she considered to be an essential job. When she asked Jack why he didn't balance his checkbook, he laughed and said he got so frustrated after being out of balance month after month, he just quit trying.

Lorraine and Jack began to compare notes on other ways they were different and it turned into a kind of game that kept them laughing while they waited for their cars. He was an early riser, she liked to sleep in. He loved prime rib, she never ate meat. She was afraid of horses, he owned three. By the time their cars were ready, they knew a great deal about each other. In spite of their differences (or maybe because of them—as I've said, opposites attract), Jack asked Lorraine out for dinner the following weekend. She agreed, but only if they could have seafood.

At dinner they began to find out that they were alike in some very important ways. They attended the same church, they were devoted to their children, and they were both hard workers. Their dinner date led to many more and now that they are married, they find their differences are an asset. The things Jack doesn't like to do, Lorraine takes care of and the things she doesn't like to do, Jack takes care of. It's a match made in . . . a car dealership.

JOIN A CHORAL GROUP

People who sing are lucky. They can be part of a chorus or choir and meet like-minded people who love getting together to make music. There are lots of opportunities to participate in a choral group, whether it's in a church choir, a community chorus, or your civic light opera.

Madeline loved to sing and had a wonderful voice. When she moved to a new community, the first thing she did was join a chorus sponsored by the city. She quickly became friends with many of the other chorus members and her social life was very busy as a result. When she was selected to sing a solo at their spring concert, Madeline was determined to be the best she could be, so she asked the conductor to work with her privately.

Thomas agreed and they made an appointment for private coaching every Wednesday night. Thomas was a hard taskmaster, and Madeline was glad she had asked for help. She knew her technique was improving rapidly and her voice was getting stronger with each passing week. She began to look forward to her lessons with more pleasure than a simple voice lesson should have warranted and realized she was falling in love with Thomas. The next week, when she went for her lesson, she looked for signs that Thomas shared her feelings and soon they were looking deeply into each other's eyes as they practiced their scales. When the lesson was over, Madeline told Thomas she was famished, and asked if he'd like to join her for some supper.

He accepted readily, and they held hands easily as they walked to a nearby restaurant. Thomas and Madelaine's relationship took a new turn that night, and when they got married, the chorus sang at their wedding.

48

GO GOLFING

Golf is a great way to meet people. That's why business-people, doctors, and other professionals make sure a game of golf is included in their weekly schedule. They know they will be spending four hours or more with the people they golf with, and that provides a lot of time for establishing a relationship.

The best way to meet new people on the golf course is to show up alone so that you will be included to complete a foursome. If you go with your own foursome, you're cutting your chances of meeting someone drastically, although hanging out in the clubhouse after the game is a good time to chat with people and dissect your game stroke by stroke as you sip a cold drink.

Donna met her husband on the golf course. She had flown to Cabo San Lucas with three of her friends, who were there for the scuba diving. Donna didn't dive, so on the days they were gone she took her golf clubs and visited one of the beautiful golf courses in the area. One day she was teamed up with three other people, a married couple who had a home on the fifth fairway, and a friend of theirs who was visiting them for the week.

The group was very friendly and down-to-earth and Donna soon felt quite comfortable. Nobody played well and nobody cared much. They were just out for the fun of it. After the game, the couple invited Donna to join them at their home for cocktails and to watch the sunset, which promised to be spectacular that evening. She accepted and followed them back to their house. Eventually she found herself on the verandah with Bob, and they began to talk. They already knew they were both from Southern California, but when they began to compare notes they learned they had attended high schools in the same league and had graduated around the same time. It wasn't long before they found they had known some of the same people.

When it came time for Donna to leave, Bob and she exchanged phone numbers and promised to contact each other when they got home. However, by the time she returned to the hotel where she and her girlfriends were staying, there was already a message from Bob inviting her to dinner the next night. They agreed to meet in the hotel lobby and their evening of dining and dancing under the stars in Mexico turned out to be the beginning of a lifetime of tee times together.

JOIN A SINGLES CLUB

There are many, many kinds of clubs open to singles only. Outdoor and sports clubs such as the Sierra Club have special groups just for singles, there are clubs for single parents only, there are singles clubs for professionals, there are singles groups sponsored by churches, there is a singles club for people with recreational vehicles, and there are dance clubs for singles.

There are a couple of different ways you can approach the idea of joining a singles club. You can join one because it will give you an opportunity to engage in an activity you particularly enjoy with other singles, or you can join one you think will put you in contact with a large number of singles of the opposite sex.

Cynthia joined a singles group of the Sierra Club for both reasons. She had learned of the group at a party she had recently attended and realized it was just what she was looking for. She wanted to find a mate who enjoyed the outdoors and was interested in protecting the environment. At the same time, she wanted to spend more time outdoors herself and didn't have anyone to go hiking with. Whether she met a mate or not, she knew she'd be doing something good for herself and for the environment.

Cynthia had been a member for several months and had participated in several of their activities when she met John on a hike in the local mountains. It was a steep climb and a very hot day and Cynthia had stopped to sit on a rock and rest for a moment. She was taking a long drink from her water bottle when John stopped and sat on a rock nearby. He uncapped his water bottle and took a drink, then made a comment to Cynthia about the heat and the altitude taking its toll on him. They rested and made small talk for a few minutes before getting up and continuing their climb. At the summit, the group broke out their bag lunches and John came and sat next to Cynthia while they ate. He had a great sense of humor and was able to poke fun at himself and life in general, something that was really important to Cynthia in a man. She looked at John a little more closely as he talked and laughed, and realized that he was quite nice-looking.

As they started down the hill, John fell in beside Cynthia and offered his hand from time to time over the steeper parts of the path. By the end of the day, Cynthia knew if he asked to see her again she would say yes.

John did ask Cynthia out and their meeting on the mountain led to a serious, long-term relationship and eventually to marriage. Cynthia and John had to drop out of the singles group of the club and join another branch when they got married, but they kept on hiking.

MIX BUSINESS WITH PLEASURE

Service clubs, such as the Chamber of Commerce, Rotary, Kiwanis, Lions, and Elks exist in almost every community and are a good way to meet people. As you work with other members to sponsor charity events, mixers, and educational workshops you will have an excellent opportunity to meet other businessmen and -women. Remember, it's always better to become actively involved than to simply attend meetings or mixers. Your contact will be more intense and the chance of a lasting relationship will increase when you sit on a committee, man a booth, or help set up or tear down for an event.

Harold joined the local Chamber of Commerce for business purposes. After attending a few mixers, he realized he wanted to be more involved and volunteered to help in whatever way they needed. The Chamber was planning their annual fund-raising event, which was to take place in a month and needed someone to round up prizes for the opportunity drawing. Harold had a great time visiting the businesses in town and getting to know the owners as he asked for donations.

When he visited a day spa in the area to see if they would donate a massage or facial, he was surprised and pleased when the owner offered a full day of services worth well over $500. Harold was so grateful he felt he ought to show his gratitude in some way, so he invited the owner of the spa to lunch. Of course, it was no great hardship for Harold, since Danielle was the most striking dark-haired beauty he had ever seen.

Danielle accepted Harold's invitation and they enjoyed each other's company very much. On an impulse, Harold asked Danielle if she would like to be his date for the fund-raising dinner, which was to be a black-tie affair. Again, she accepted.

The night of the dinner, Danielle looked stunning in a crimson strapless gown. Harold was awestruck the entire evening, and could barely take his eyes off her. Besides being beautiful, Danielle was a savvy businesswoman and a delightful companion. Soon Harold and Danielle were a twosome at all the Chamber events, and when they became engaged the announcement made the front page of the Chamber's monthly newsletter.

LEARN TEN MAGIC WORDS

The best way to meet your mate is to say these ten words to everyone you meet—your friends, co-workers, doctor, dentist, barber, hairdresser, minister, boss, landlord, tenant, instructor, realtor, banker, stockbroker, housekeeper, travel agent—anyone who knows you even casually. I've shared these ten magic words with many, many singles, and the result has been many, many lasting relationships.

What are they? "You must know someone who would be perfect for me."

Although people may know you're single, they don't necessarily know that you're searching for a mate, and it would never occur to them to fix you up. When you let them know you're looking, they mentally go down the list of people they know who would be a good match for you.

The following story is a perfect example of how this works.

Kay was tired of carrying around twenty extra pounds and decided to do something about it. She went to a weight loss clinic where she was assigned to Teresa, a weight loss counselor. As Teresa took Kay's measurements, she asked her if she were married or single. Kay told her she was single and dying to meet someone who wasn't afraid to be in a committed relationship. Kay said, "You must know someone who would be perfect for me."

Teresa jumped up from measuring Kay's thigh and said, "I can't believe this! I know the perfect person for you. His name is Neal. He lives in Chicago, but I can have him call you." Kay was a little shocked but said, "Great! Tell him to call me."

Kay, who lived in Cleveland, got a call from Neal the next day. After a couple of weeks talking on the phone, Neal asked

Kay if he could fly to Cleveland and take her to dinner. Kay couldn't wait to meet him and cheerfully agreed. When they met at the airport, they felt an instant connection and hugged warmly. They both knew at that moment this was the person they would spend the rest of their lives with. They've been married ten years and are still madly in love.

I know of couples who have met in such unusual places as prison, in group therapy, at the shooting range, playing craps in Las Vegas, skydiving, bungee jumping, getting a traffic ticket, and rock climbing. I also know of couples who have met doing such mundane things as washing their car, taking their cat to the vet, having their carpet shampooed, or getting a haircut. As I've said before, life is an adventure. Keep your eyes and ears open, because you never know when you'll meet your perfect mate!

AFTERWORD

Although you have come to the end of this book, I hope it's just the beginning of a lifetime of happiness for you.

You deserve to have a mate you can love and cherish with all your heart and who loves you in the same way. Living with a mate and loving them "as long as you both shall live" can be the most challenging and rewarding experience you'll ever have. The kind of communion that comes from having someone at your side to share your successes and failures, the good times and the bad, cannot be equaled.

As human beings, we are all a work in progress. Unlike a painting, a poem, or a novel, our development never ends. It is an ongoing process that can always be added to, but never completed. We must always keep growing and learning so that we can love more deeply, relate more intimately, communicate more effectively, and enjoy ourselves more fully.

By now you should have a journal filled with personal insights about your life experiences. Re-read the entries you have made on a regular basis and keep adding to your journal as your life continues to unfold.

With the knowledge you have gained and the willingness to put it into action, you can become one of the perfect couples that others call "lucky." By now, however, you should know what I've known all my life: luck is nothing more than hard work that has finally paid off.

As you proceed with your plan of action, you will be quite busy, but don't expect instant results. If you try something once and it doesn't work, give it another chance. Don't assume it will never work. Sometimes the timing just isn't exactly right and the next time will bring you the results you are looking for.

It's also important to remember to relax and enjoy the process. There's a saying, "Life is what happens while you're making other plans." Don't let life pass you by while you search for your mate. If your life is busy and fulfilling without a mate, you will automatically be a more attractive prospect than someone who is waiting for a mate to create fulfillment in them.

Whatever you do, don't ever give up your search for the perfect mate. I know the man or woman of your dreams is close by, waiting to be discovered by you. Never give up believing in fairy tales. It is possible to live happily ever after. It will happen to you.

I would love to hear your success story and how you've put into practice what you've just learned. You can write to me at P.O. Box 1511, Lake Forest, CA 92630 or visit or e-mail me at my Web site: www.lightyourfire.com.

I wish you all the love, happiness, and fulfillment that you deserve.

Love,

Ellen

You may be eligible for a free honeymoon vacation. Simply write a brief account about how Ellen's sage advice from *Single No More* helped you and your perfect mate become engaged and send it to Renaissance Media along with a proof of purchase of this book. All entries must be postmarked by February 1, 2000 to qualify. No one employed by or affiliated with Renaissance Media is eligible. Ellen will select the winning entry and announce it on national television by February 14, 2000. Contest winner and mate may be invited to appear on television with Ellen. This offer is not intended to violate any state or federal laws and is not applicable in any state where the law prohibits offers of this nature.

Good luck!

Mail or fax entries to:

RENAISSANCE MEDIA
5858 WILSHIRE BLVD., SUITE 200
LOS ANGELES, CA 90036
ATTN: HONEYMOON VACATION
FAX: (323) 939-6436
NO PHONE CALLS PLEASE